Anita Bhogle is a post-graduate in s   ......, and in management (IIM-A) and a professed 'quant' person. She effortlessly made the transition to qualitative research, to account planning, to even scripting and producing TV commercials but still retains a love for wicked level sudokus and the keyboard. She started her career at Contract Advertising, was head of strategic planning and research at FCBUlka and founded Prosearch Consultants which owes its name to her background in research.

At Prosearch, she conceived *The Winning Way*, a presentation that married learnings from management and sport. In the fifteen years that it has been invited to the heart of corporate India, she has made it synonymous with its genre in India, constantly revising it and ensuring that it remains relevant at all times. Her innate analytical skills combined with Harsha's ringside view of sport have made it a unique offering where two people present in their own styles.

Harsha Bhogle has had an unusual career since graduating in chemical engineering from Osmania University, Hyderabad, and then completing a post-graduate programme in management from IIM-A. After working in advertising, he moved into sports media, traversing its many paths and displaying the different skills each demanded, before being recognized as the face and the voice of Indian cricket; even having a talent show (*Hunt for Harsha*) named after him. His exposure to the world of management allowed him to bring different insights to cricket commentary where he has been part of over a hundred test matches, over 400 one-day games and more T20 games than can be remembered. He has hosted the finals of World Cups and World T20s (and on one occasion the FIFA World Cup) and is one of India's most-read columnists.

His as much a television person as a pioneer in the digital medium. His Twitter following places him among the top few in the world in sports media and his blogs on CricBuzz touched a 100 million views in the first few months of their appearance.

It is this marriage, quite literally, that has produced one of India's most admired corporate speaking programmes.

The

WINNING
WAY 2.0

Learnings from Sports for Managers

ANITA BHOGLE &
HARSHA BHOGLE

BUSINESS

An imprint of Penguin Random House

PENGUIN BUSINESS

USA | Canada | UK | Ireland | Australia
New Zealand | India | South Africa | China

Penguin Business is part of the Penguin Random House group of companies
whose addresses can be found at global.penguinrandomhouse.com

Published by Penguin Random House India Pvt. Ltd
4th Floor, Capital Tower 1, MG Road,
Gurugram 122 002, Haryana, India

First published by Westland Ltd 2011
Revised edition published by Westland Publications Ltd 2017
Published in Penguin Business by Penguin Random House India 2022

ISBN 9780143458494

Designed by SŪRYA, New Delhi

www.penguin.co.in

To our fathers, R.S. Kulkarni and A.D. Bhogle, whom we remember every day and who so influenced us. How we would have loved to present them this.

To our mothers, Lily Kulkarni and Shalini Bhogle, in whose lap we first sought, and received, shelter and who have always been there for us.

Contents

Foreword

Sport and business have much in common. Competitiveness, dynamism, uncertainty, strategy and execution, and above all, leadership and team work.

As businesses and corporations take on newer and greater global challenges, they will have to rapidly and efficiently disseminate best practices to their people in a decentralized yet effective manner. Building capacity and speedily bridging competence gaps will have to be done in unique and innovative ways. Anita and Harsha Bhogle attempt such an innovation in a most outstanding way—by drawing out business lessons from sport in a gripping book.

I have loved sport since childhood, especially cricket!

This book took me down memory lane. It brought all my memories of sport and business alive. With the advent of the Indian Premier League (IPL), my wife Nita and I have become more closely associated with cricket. We have ourselves learned a great deal in business from this association.

Harsha has been an integral part of Indian cricket's

growth. He is part of an ecosystem which has put India on the global map. Indian cricket is now globally respected and admired—thanks to the important role that Harsha has played in the process.

Harsha has made us romance and understand cricket. His insightful mind has never ceased to amaze me. His immaculate analysis of the game brings new perspectives to one's mind. His personal relationships with great sportsmen have given him unique insights into the game and the minds of its masters. His ability to do parallel processing of information and convert it into golden nuggets, garnished by eloquent language, is truly astonishing!

His partnership with Anita is a great example of how two people can work together. Her sharp, incisive mind, honed by many years in the advertising world, is at the heart of the work they do and you can see her touch all along. She is the genuine modern all-rounder and as they advocate in the book, they set up a goal for each other to score.

This book, *The Winning Way*, is a great collation of Anita and Harsha's knowledge of sport.

They have gathered little pearls of wisdom at the intersection of sport, business, cinema and life, which can be found on almost every page of this book.

Reading this book is as pleasurable an experience as listening to a commentary—indeed, more so. The language has a beautiful flow and the writing is replete with appropriate examples and anecdotes. Their trademark touch is remarkably refreshing.

The Winning Way is an invigorating read. Understanding the business world through the lens of sport is stimulating and energizing. The book has expressively and compellingly laid out the 'ground rules' of winning!

This book is a great gift to ambitious aspirants from the corporate as well as the entrepreneurship worlds. I do hope the values and lessons derived get well entrenched in the global leaders of the future.

March 2011   MUKESH D. AMBANI
Mumbai

Why This Book

I believe that in an athlete's life, winning is important, but, the journey is more meaningful! The constant pursuit of overcoming one's own limitations and always challenging the part of you that says you will not or cannot win! I am convinced that everybody has, at some time in their life, faced an equivalent. Something that feels insurmountable. My, perhaps unsolicited, advice is to enjoy the ride! Let's face it, roller coasters are far more thrilling than merry go rounds!

—Abhinav Bindra

Eight years ago we started a motivational series called 'The Winning Way'. It is a workshop that draws upon lessons from sport and applies them to organisations. It talks about champion sports people and winning teams in all kinds of sport, what they do, the practices they follow, the habits they cultivate—and it tries to draw parallels with corporate issues and situations. 'The Winning Way' stems from our deep-rooted belief that the formula for winning remains the same whether you are a sportsman, a musician, a financial planner, a pharmaceutical salesman or a housewife. Since the principles behind success remain the same, anyone using them should be able to reach their full potential and succeed.

Since 'The Winning Way' has received several repeat requests from Microsoft, HSBC, Unilever, Glaxo SmithKline, Aventis, Cadbury's, Marico, Castrol, Colgate and the like, we have felt encouraged enough to put together this book. It consists of our reflections on winning, what constitutes a winner and, to put it simply, how all of us can win.

The past few years have been a continuous learning process for us. We have witnessed up close, the rise and fall of several cricket captains, the emergence of Twenty20 as an interesting innovation in the sport, the metamorphosis of Indian cricket under Ganguly and Dhoni and the domination of Australia in all forms of the game. We have seen many sports persons up close through their ups and downs. While doing all of this, through our workshops we have also interacted with stalwarts from industry, many of them passionate followers of sports themselves, and this interaction has enriched the dialogue. This book then, while making no claims about being a complete handbook on winning, is the collation of our collective learning – from the world of sport and the world of business.

In 2004, along with CNBC, we produced a novel programme called *Masterstrokes* where every episode saw a cricketer and a corporate head discuss various aspects of winning. It reinforced our belief that there was much that managers could learn from sport.

Over the last eight years, we have travelled across countries and cities, speaking about winning and what it takes to win. This book draws from our work spanning close to 300 sessions for 150 companies across almost all sectors. There were old economy companies trying to cope with market changes and simultaneously, with a changed, new generation; there were companies that had issues arising from growth and globalisation; some were reeling under the burden of their own growth and some companies were in businesses so new that they didn't know how different their tomorrow would look from today. The one thread that was common to such diversely-placed businesses was that they were all keen to win.

We also realized as we engaged with these supposedly diverse businesses that whatever your product or service may be, in today's world where technology and processes can be outsourced, plant and machinery imported and finance acquired very easily, it finally boils down to people. Since these people are drawn from the same common pool, it is only team culture and environment, leadership and vision, attitude towards change and occasional failure, that determine team performance.

The years 2008-09 saw the dark cloud of recession hover over the economy, bringing with it salary cuts, pink slips and tremendous insecurity. This was a huge challenge for everyone, but especially for new entrants to the corporate world who had come in with dreams of a boom time and also for HR managers in sectors like IT and BPOs with a very young employee profile. Senior managers too told us that they needed to hang on to their jobs since there weren't that many available for their kind of profile.

As we made this journey, interestingly, we found that winning was not this 'one size fits all' cloak of invincibility. It wasn't a trophy or medal that would look just as good in any display or a rose that would smell just as sweet in any boardroom. Winning came in different shades and sizes. The ambitions of companies and their mission statements varied dramatically. The big realisation was that size does matter but that size isn't everything. That you could have goals—and sometimes need to have goals—other than being number one. Also, that the problems that winners have are often bigger and more complicated than those of the also-rans. Over eight years we have seen the business environment changing and along with it we have seen corporate India start to approach success very differently. With many of the companies, we did an exercise where we asked executives to analyse which international cricket team their own team resembled and which one they aspired to be like. In many cases, the first hurdle was for the executives to figure out what exactly was meant by 'teams' as new- age organisational structures, global reporting relationships and other such concepts have given an all new twist to this term. That sorted out, many teams aspired to be

Australia, the unquestioned leader. But as India started winning, first under Ganguly and then Dhoni, more and more people rooted for India as the team they wanted to emulate. Interestingly, it was also the time when L. N. Mittal and Ratan Tata made it to the covers of international magazines.

We have often wondered if in recent years the state of the Indian economy and the state of Indian cricket seem to be closely correlated. Is it a mere coincidence that Arcelor and Corus happened around the same time as India's Twenty20 victory in 2007? Would Ganguly and Dhoni be at ease discussing leadership issues with Nandan Nilekani and Sunil Bharti Mittal—on how to motivate a young India with global dreams and an attitude to match? When we started our careers in 1985, nobody challenged the Levers and the Tatas—quite in the way that Indian cricket was happy with respectable draws against England or the West Indies.

Those pre-liberalisation times were uncomplicated and young executives like us were naïve. Dreams were limited and constraints were more talked about than ambition. Life was simple, media options limited and job security was paramount to most people. There were a few good brands and a few employers people aspired to work with. As young advertising professionals, we were account planning, media planning and servicing people all rolled into one. There was no need for specialisation. When we read retail audit reports and noted small changes in brand share, the boss would ask 'Grown by volume or value?' That was our first lesson, that winning on paper was one thing. Winning in the marketplace, through actual volume growth, was something else.

Today, the stakes attached to winning are very high, whether in sport or in business. People see the growth of cricket in India mostly in financial terms, for that has been the most dramatic rise. But the world over, the game itself has evolved by leaps and bounds. The contest between bat and ball is the same, but elements like fitness, speed and strategy have become critical and changed the face of the game beyond recognition. New variants of the game like Twenty20 have emerged. With corporate entry into franchises, the game has become even more exciting and challenging.

We are therefore in a strange situation today. On the one hand, it's a 'perform or perish' kind of pressure situation. On the other hand, leaders are also constantly being told to nurture and empower their teams, understand the whole person rather than merely assess the young man or woman at the workplace. So, can the hand that cracks the whip also be the reassuring hand on an over burdened shoulder? Winning today is about finding the balance between being encouraging and being ruthless. Unlike in other areas, winning in sport gives a high not only to those who play, but also to people like us who follow sport. It's a high that is cherished and talked about long after the event. There are few things in life more inspiring and motivating than sport. This book attempts to share some insights on winning through examples from the fascinating world of real-life champions.

Why 2.0?

At several points in *The Winning Way* we have advocated a '*Chalo karke dekhte hain!*' (Let's give it a shot!) attitude. Embrace opportunity for you never know where it takes you. It is exactly this attitude that prompted us to write *The Winning Way* the first time around. People seemed to be getting back to reading and after having conducted about 300 live sessions of *The Winning Way*, we had quite a few things to share. To be completely honest, we had wondered at the time if an economically-priced paperback would lower the demand for live sessions. But we went ahead nonetheless and in 2016, by which time the book had turned five years old, sales had crossed 100,000 copies and we were nudging 500 sessions, we were pleasantly surprised to find that clients who had invited us for live sessions earlier continued, not just to invite us but also to present copies to participants It set us thinking. And around the same time we ran into fellow writer and IIMA alumnus, Ravi Subramanian at a party. Ravi, unlike us has turned almost fulltime author and has gone on to write many books. Ravi had no idea how many copies we had sold but seemed to think that our book had an advantage; it had longevity. As long as sport continued to inspire and capture people's imagination, *The Winning Way* would continue to resonate. While that was a delightful thought, we also realized that the world had moved on substantially and so if the book needed to remain relevant and contemporary (something that is so critical in today's changing world and something we never tire stressing on both in the book and in sessions), it needed to be refreshed.

Social media really took off after we released *The Winning Way*. It gave us a chance to engage with readers. Many wrote in telling us what parts they liked, how they revisited the book from time to time, how it had uplifted them. Business leaders made notes and shared them with their teams. The response was phenomenal. They obviously took us more seriously than we took ourselves! A big thank you to all of you for partnering with us and enriching *The Winning Way*.

So here's *The Winning Way 2.0*. With two new chapters and many more stories and analyses in all the earlier ones.

Two words that held centre-stage in the last five years have been innovation and disruption. Joining a start-up if not starting one yourself became fashionable and aspirational. Suddenly, all assumptions were being questioned and young entrepreneurs became more in demand at conferences than grey-haired folks. The IPL, from being a fledgling tournament evolved into a full-blown case study in innovation. As we like to say, in a sense cricket disrupted itself! Not all good players could necessarily adapt while names that weren't seriously being talked about started fetching fancy price tags at the auction. While the longer formats continue to be played, the game has changed forever. The biggest innovation in sport has given us much to learn from and merited an entire chapter.

With more and more leagues like the IPL cropping up, cricketers became freelance, hawking their craft from team to team. They now identify more with the role than the side they are playing for. Many pundits seem to think that is going to be how the workplace will look in the future. What does that do to the idea of a team, to team bonding and loyalty?

Gen Y was now becoming a more and more significant part of the workforce. They represented a new, confident India wanting to take on the world. As wrestler Sushil Kumar observed, 'Earlier athletes went to participate in the Olympics, now they go to win medals.' While cricket continued to remain the biggest draw, sports like badminton, wrestling and shooting saw new champions and a lot more interest. It was heartening to see people cancelling social commitments to watch P. V. Sindhu and Dipa Karmakar in the Olympics finals.

While more champions emerged, we were shocked to see the fall of some of yesterday's heroes like Lance Armstrong and to an extent, Tiger Woods and the ban on teams like Chennai Super Kings and Rajasthan Royals.

Match-fixing raised its ugly head but we have seen more reform than ever before.

It is always distressing when the reason for a fall is not related to performance. It makes you wonder if all their earlier achievements now amount to nothing. It makes you think about success differently. We have put down some of our thoughts in the chapter 'What price, winning?'

Despite the aberrations, sport continues to be one of the most positive and inspiring forces of our times. In many ways it mirrors society and shapes lives. It gives joy and hope while uniting people and nations. There is so much that one can learn from playing and watching sport. We have tried our best to share this with you.

The Business of Winning

An athlete cannot run with money in his pockets. He must run with hope in his heart and dreams in his head.

—Emil Zatopek

Television, the greatest ally of sport, creates dramatic images of adrenalin-fuelled athletes making a courageous, even frantic, race towards victory. There are few sights more moving than victory, or brave defeat, or indeed heroic effort. Remember Sachin Tendulkar braving the sandstorm and the opposition at Sharjah in 1998, or Anil Kumble bowling with a broken jaw in Antigua in 2002, or Misbah-ul-huq down on the ground after having tried so hard in the first World Twenty20 championship in 2007? Or indeed Virat Kohli straining to pull off an impossible win at Adelaide in 2014!

But winning and losing are no more than a step in a much longer journey; a crucial step, but just one step. Teams that journey better take that step better, far more easily. Teams that flounder and lose their way in between may reach the finish line, but in all likelihood, with someone ahead of them.

So why do some teams win more often than others? Why are some teams more mercurial, capable of astonishing performances one day and appalling ones the next? Is there a formula to winning that only some possess? Or is it out there for everybody to follow but only some are inclined to reach out for it? Is there a culture to winning? If there is, why do some teams embrace it with passion while others merely look at it from a distance?

The Winning Cycle

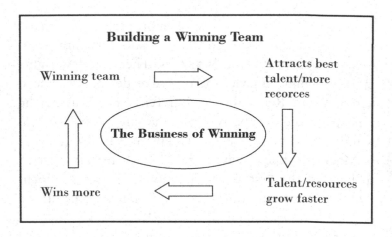

The ideal situation for teams would be to search for that often elusive cycle of winning. The good news is that it exists maybe more like Boyle's Law, with conditions attached, than like the basic laws of mathematics that are rigid and therefore, more universal! Many teams around the world seem able to create such a cycle and keep it going.

Good players like playing in winning teams and as teams create an aura around themselves, youngsters dream of being part of the legacy. Inevitably therefore, winning teams attract the best talent and because they create a climate where talent is allowed to flourish, players get better faster and that contributes to winning more often. Manchester United, Real Madrid and the Los Angeles Lakers, for example, seem to have created that cycle. Australia's cricket team seemed able to do it ... and when we were passing out of IIM-A in the mid-eighties, Hindustan Unilever (then known as Hindustan Lever) had a similar aura. The best graduates went there, they learnt faster and it became a breeding ground for new corporate leaders. As a result, a day into the placement season we looked at the guys who had made it there with a mixture of awe and confusion. They were one of us but suddenly seemed to be a couple of inches taller!

When asked what creates this aura, Nitin Paranjpe, then MD and CEO, Hindustan Unilever Limited (HUL) elaborated, 'First and foremost is the capacity to demonstrate that you can win consistently. But that is not enough. You could win and still not have the aura. And that is because of how you go about it. One aspect of that is the means you use to win, the values you demonstrate. The second aspect is how you are seen by others—whether you are a thought leader, whether you have a clear point of view about the future well before the others. The success that you thus achieve feeds on itself. But winning today is not enough. You need to win today and tomorrow.'[1]

That tomorrow can look different from today is truer now than ever before. When change comes, it can shake even the biggest and the strongest and can have repercussions on established institutions like what the T20 format has done to the other forms of cricket or what startups are doing to corporate giants. We asked one of our nephews who recently quit a job with a Big Four accounting firm to join a start-up, how difficult it was to chuck a fancy salary, and a visiting card, for something that was a little more than an idea. The young man just smiled and shook his head and said, 'Very easy!' Today Google is the most attractive employer for Gen Y—a company that not only provides the best facilities at the workplace but also the best environment and encouragement for aspiring entrepreneurs.

It presents a major challenge to organisations and especially to managers who have become very good at doing things a certain way. To illustrate this, in the context of T20 cricket, a ball on a perfect length just outside off stump, a good ball in test cricket, becomes an easily hittable ball in T20. And so a bowler has to cast aside an old definition of a good ball for a different form of the game. Skill in one form isn't an indicator of success in another.

In corporate India where movement is much freer than it is in predominantly inter-country sport, companies seek to be employers of choice almost as much they seek market share. They know that if you create the right environment, talent will flourish. Organisations rarely have to tell talented, driven players to perform. More often, they just need to make them feel good. Sourav Ganguly would never have had to go to Sachin Tendulkar and say, 'Sachin, please, we need a fifty from you. The team really needs it!' Tendulkar probably wants to score that fifty, or hundred, more than anyone else, but if the atmosphere in the dressing room is not conducive, his mind is likely to be full of negative thoughts, as indeed it can be in organisations that employ ambitious men and women. When companies start becoming completely goal-centric and forget that it is people who produce results, they struggle. Just as players in good teams enjoy going to compete, so should people enjoy going to work. This is only one reason why the human resource function is such an important aspect of winning teams! Human resource management becomes even more important during tough times, prompting N. R. Narayana Murthy to remark, 'At Infosys we say at 9.00 a.m. when every one of our people is working, the marketcap may be whatever it is, 15 or 16 in these tough days, but at 6.15 or 7.00 p.m. or maybe 9.00 p.m., when the last of us has gone home, the marketcap is zero.'[2]

In his wonderful book, *The Winner Within*, the former coach of the Los Angeles Lakers, Pat Riley, writes of the great bonding in the team that helped in winning the NBA title in 1980. However, towards the end of the season a young man called Magic Johnson, soon to take the world by storm, came off the substitute bench and played a leadership role. At the start of the next season the team got drawn into the rivalry, partially media created, between Johnson and the erstwhile star Kareem Abdul Jabbar. A battle of one-upmanship can be good in a team up to a point, since a player's individual score contributes to the team score anyway. Beyond a point, the objective can be to outdo one another rather than do what is best for the team and that can be disastrous for morale and results. The Lakers, now a team in disarray, made one of the fastest exits a defending champion has made going out in the first round of the playoffs in 1981. Two match-winners had collided and taken the team down with them, when a harmonious environment might have had the two champions standing shoulder-to-shoulder.

What Causes Winning Cycles to Break

Often discord can be produced by players who put individual goals ahead of what is in the interest of the team. Such players are not too difficult to spot. The forward who looks for the dramatic goal from an impossible angle rather than slide it to an unmarked teammate; the batsman who slows down in quest of a hundred in a one-day international and ends up costing his team an extra twenty runs; the publicity-seeking boss who claims credit for a great product launch. While it is vital that players, medical reps, real-estate sales executives, anyone really, have personal goals for we would be robots without them, there are times when teams get into trouble when a collection of such strictly individual goals derails the team ethic.

So as you can see, winning cycles can break if there is discord, or if young blood, instead of competing, stays on the bench for too long. If there is no room for fresh talent, teams can stagnate in performance and in thought. Players need to be challenged all the time, it is what keeps them hungry and excited, and like nature, organisations must have mechanisms not only for nurturing but also culling. Australia remained strong because they had a very rigorous, almost brutal, exit policy. When Ian Healy wanted to finish in front of his home crowd, he was told he couldn't because Adam Gilchrist was ready. Steve Waugh wanted to finish his career with a win in India in 2004 but was told he wasn't going to stay that long. At the first sign of decline in Gilchrist, the word must have gone out too. When Wayne Rooney and Cristiano Ronaldo arrived at Manchester United, Ruud van Nistelroy was bid goodbye and Ryan Giggs was found more often on the bench than in the field. When young players realize they are getting an opportunity because of a stringent exit policy, they also know that they can't linger when their time comes.

Too often teams spend time retaining talent, whereas

culling it when the time comes is a ruthless, but just as necessary, way of keeping a winning cycle going. When teams dither, hanging on to players because of sentiment or as a reward, they run the risk of getting stuck with a lot of players on the declining side of a product life cycle curve and end up losing a lot of players simultaneously. Also, the message going out to the younger replacements is that the individual matters more than the team. That is where Australia has been good over the years; nurturing players and backing them to the hilt while, at the same time, recognising the need to create hungry teams. In contrast, the general feeling was that Jayasuriya and Kapil Dev were allowed to hang around a bit longer than was necessary.

The manner in which an organization handles the exit or retirement of its stars tells us a thing or two about its team culture and to what extent it allows the cult of the individual to flourish. Saying goodbye to legends always involves a great deal of emotion and teams that have had a Tendulkar, a Lara or a Steve Waugh be an integral part of them for so long, would struggle to come to terms with a time without them around. Interestingly, the BCCI in a fanboy moment declared that Sachin alone would take a decision on his retirement (continue to play as long as he wished to). It would be interesting to debate how differently Cricket Australia or indeed any of India's large corporate giants would have handled the retirement of one of its stalwarts.

In a booming economy, when employees move around

with offer letters in their pockets, companies run the risk of losing their best people while the 'bottom quartile' for lack of other opportunities remains in the company. If this process carries on for a couple of cycles, even if you replenish the team through good, external hires it could seriously lower the standard of the team and that too at a much higher cost. No wonder HR managers have coined the term 'positive attrition'—happy to see the bottom leaving, making way for better performers.

Another issue that arises when the best leave and the lowest performers get left behind is that those who stay in the company longest (not out of choice!) start believing that they are the most loyal and in fact the custodians of the brand making it difficult for them to accept negative feedback. The only way out therefore is regular and systematic culling and replacing with fresh talent from outside. There are still the public sector companies and some benevolent private sector employers who continue to boast that they don't sack anyone but in today's competitive world they will need to cull to be performance-driven.

A steady inflow of fresh and young talent becomes potent only when that talent is encouraged to think and is empowered to express their views. McKinsey makes it obligatory for its young managers to 'agree to disagree'. Getting people to express their views leads to greater accountability. Once a decision is taken and the whole team comes on board, it is difficult to pass the buck. Bharat Puri, former MD of Cadbury India Ltd. believes that great communication is a hallmark of winning teams and that depends on whether it is the organisation's culture to promote open communication.[3]

There might be shifts in technology, or demographics, or government policy as well that could cause winning cycles to break. With the entry of Amazon and Flipkart, it became unviable for brick-and-mortar bookstores like Borders and Crossword. The inability to see the arrival of affordable dual SIM phones arrested Nokia's great journey. In sport, great Test teams could look out of place in a Twenty20(T20) environment for example. Players born into an atmosphere of not letting a bowler get them out discovered that they had to play with a different set of values; that being out after belting a quick 30 was more valuable than denying a bowler a wicket and making 35 in 50 balls. In such a situation, teams can look dated and in desperate need of newer players with more contemporary skills. At other times, you may need to change coaches, or for that matter consultants, who might be stuck in a time capsule. When T20 cricket first arrived, the players hadn't played it, but coaches hadn't experienced it either. So their traditional role, which was to impart knowledge based on their own experience, was under threat. To give a slightly different example, when hockey went the astro-turf way, with hard hitting and quick movements, India's coaches were still stuck on grass, trying to play a beautiful, dribbling and skills-oriented but obsolete game!

Sometimes teams that win consistently at one level

find it difficult to win at the next level. This inability to take the game to the next level or raise the game could be talent-related or simply a result of being content at remaining a big fish in a smaller pond and not really aspiring for a bigger pond. If good is good enough, why bother about getting to great?

So as we have seen, teams need to cull with the same intensity with which they need to nurture. The best teams are those that back their players all the way, but when they find that players can no longer contribute for various reasons, (becoming irrelevant is but one of those), they don't waste time in letting them go.

Iconic brands, otherwise, might end up becoming 'dad's brands' and we saw that when India's economy was opened up and became market driven. Companies that had thrived on licenses and monopolies and didn't really care about the customer, virtually perished. For a long time the Indian two- wheeler market was dominated by the scooter and when we were young, bikes were for the somewhat reckless, wannabe young men. Scooters had stepneys in case you got a flat, while bikers didn't care too much about these things. The scooter was a solid middle-class possession and Bajaj was the god who could deliver one to you. Waitlists stretched for ten years and so Bajaj really didn't need to compete with anybody. Then Hero Honda started a revolution—riding a scooter became terribly passé, you didn't get flat tyres anymore and Bajaj was forced to compete. The iconic Rahul Bajaj gave way to a younger generation who manufactured motorcycles which competed admirably with Hero Honda. Bajaj culled in time or else they could have ended up with the equivalent of classy Test players in a T20 team.

While Bajaj was able to re-establish the cycle, leading camera companies were unable to prevent the advance of the cell phone that took photographs. A dramatic change in technology broke the winning cycle for them as it did for Australia in the early years of T20 cricket.

Apart from such major changes there are others than can cause a winning cycle to break. Teams can sometimes take their foot off the pedal, lose the focus on winning and let faults build up (while they are winning) until they become critical and almost impossible to conceal. Some people believe that Colgate-Palmolive fell into this trap in the late nineties when they let HUL outflank them for a while with the launch of the Pepsodent and Close-Up brands which were targeted specifically at youth. As it turned out, it was just the wake-up call Colgate needed to return strongly. Indeed, in the early days of their long association, Colgate-Palmolive's brief to their advertising agency Rediffusion was—'Don't change anything.' One got the impression that Colgate-Palmolive didn't exactly know which part of their winning formula was working and so didn't want to change anything for fear of removing the successful elements. We have also heard of businesses that lost energy and enthusiasm after the initial excitement was over and they got into the consolidation phase. Middle-order batsmen have a different role to play and need to leverage the great start provided by the openers.

Sometimes good teams can take winning for granted, delude themselves into thinking they merely need to turn up to win; they let the arrogance remain but let the work ethic dwindle. There was always a suspicion that this was the case with the teams that followed the great West Indies outfits of the late seventies, eighties and early nineties; the arrogance remained, the work ethic vanished!

To prevent teams from starting to think that they have 'arrived', Deep Kalra, founder and CEO, MakeMyTrip.com, (himself reinventing his company after a heady start) suggests that one think of success as a moving target. As he puts it, 'The trick is tell yourself every day that all this "success" business is firstly relative ... it helps to look at other companies (in his case such as Apple, Facebook, Google and Amazon), or the entrepreneurs behind them and secondly, that success is mercurial ... it can go as soon as it comes. Especially once you have public market stock.'[4]

Winning cycles, we think are getting shorter. Earlier, number 1 brands had a longer run at the top. Bajaj and then Hero in two-wheelers, Philips in electricals, Rajesh Khanna and then Amitabh Bachchan in films ruled in their categories for several years. Now trends keep changing and most categories have five or six brands closely competing with each other. 2015 already saw the return of scooters; making up for 30 per cent of the two-wheeler market led by Honda. It's no longer lonely at the top!

To return to winning. Probably the biggest reason some teams win more often than others is that they know how to win. Many years ago, Michel Platini, one of the finest football players in the world, said the team that would win the soccer World Cup would be the team that knew how to. You might scoff at this simplistic statement. On close examination, you'll probably come around to the conclusion that there is a lot of truth in it.

Why Some Teams Can't Keep the Winning Cycle Going

Teams that don't win very often, invariably don't know what to do when placed in a winning position. They freeze. They choke. As do teams that are so obsessed with the idea of winning that they grow tense and often stop thinking when a calm mind would have taken them home. Maybe there is a story then behind South Africa's misadventures in the World Cup. After a dramatic re-entry to international cricket in 1992, they often found themselves in winning positions and threw the win away; never more obvious than in the dramatic 1999 World Cup semi-final when they had tied the score and needed only a single from four balls. First, Allan Donald charged out for a non-existent single and almost ran himself out and then Lance Klusener, who was hitting the ball wherever he wanted to, hit the ball and ran. Donald didn't. The two players froze, with victory waiting at their doorstep.

The fear of winning can sometimes be greater than the fear of losing! That is why winning a Test series against Australia in 2008 was seen by South Africans as being as important as winning the rugby World Cup on a dramatic night in 1995; the beast, which for so long was an annoying tenant, was finally off their back. Yet, when it came to cricket World Cup events, the tenant inevitably reappeared. For a team with an outstanding win percentage in bilateral series, they continued to choke in mega world events. As a consequence, their obsession with getting results at times derailed the performance that could get them there in the first place.

We saw that in the World Cup of 2015 too when South Africa stormed through to the semi-finals before the familiar demons returned to choke them. We saw that too with Pakistan whose record against India in World Cup games, as opposed to normal bilateral or multi-country tournaments, is difficult to believe. When asked about it, Shoaib Akhtar, himself part of a couple of derailed campaigns, said they thought too much about the game, suddenly planned differently whereas their natural Instinct might have taken them home. New Zealand too, played breathtaking, fearless cricket, all the way to the final and then, all of a sudden, seemed a different side. Maybe the fear of the big day had arrived for them too.

A young player growing up in that otherwise excellent

South African side would have inherited the tension associated with winning on a big day. On the other hand, a young man learning his trade in Australia's awesome teams through the mid-nineties and the first decade of the new millennium, would have seen how senior players were focused on winning. A young man like Michael Clarke, sharing the dressing room with the likes of Shane Warne, Glenn McGrath, Ricky Ponting, Mathew Hayden and Adam Gilchrist would have learnt how to win and how to close matches, as part of his grooming in international cricket. An equally talented young man like Mohammed Ashraful of Bangladesh, growing up in a losing environment, could never have learnt the discipline of winning. Self-belief is an essential aspect of development and if you are not winning, you'll never acquire it. We are sure our friends in HUL, many of whom have gone on to have outstanding careers, will have a similar story of learning to tell. As indeed will companies that failed to close deals; either because they thought they already had them in the bag, or because they didn't quite know what to do at that crucial last stage.

In 2006, Australia went to Bangladesh at the end of a very long and tiring season. The players were exhausted (Brett Lee famously said there was no fuel in the tank, only fumes), they wanted to be home and it seemed a rare occasion to see an Australian team wanting to put its feet up rather than play cricket. They were not as intense as they normally were and maybe took things for granted. (Another vital truth about sport and live television is that if you take things for granted it can be quite unforgiving.) At the end of the first day, Bangladesh were 355 for 5, a situation that was entirely unexpected and one they had scarcely found themselves in before. To our astonishment, their captain Habibul Bashar said at the press conference later in the evening that if they scored another hundred runs they would be 'safe'. We were astounded but you can understand where Bashar was coming from. If, all your life, you have aspired not to lose, being 'safe' is an accomplishment.

The next day they had Australia down at 145 for 6 and Adam Gilchrist was at the press conference. 'We're in a bit of a hole and need to figure out how to win from here,' he said, and in that moment, you could see the difference between the two sides. The underdogs, through years of defeat, were unaware that they were in a winning position. Opportunity had knocked on their door, they didn't recognize it, because they weren't ready for it. The champions, on the other hand were always moving ahead, they were focussing on victory. It came as no surprise when Australia won, despite the fact that they had defeat staring them in the face on more than one occasion during the course of the match. Bangladesh was left wondering whether it could have been a turning point in their cricketing history! This is why it is often said that to be a champion, you need big match temperament.

You'll find too that organisations that can't quite 'close matches' spend the rest of their lives wondering what might have been and getting frustrated when they find that the world doesn't really have time for their kind. Quite apart from this example, you'll find that good teams are able to put the past behind them and focus on the present; to accept the situation as given and not grieve over what might have been. A couple of youngsters in the Rajasthan Royals team that won the first IPL said their captain Shane Warne was always telling them, 'How can we win from here?' Sachin Tendulkar is like that, and so was Anil Kumble—always trying to look ahead rather than worrying about why they got into a bad situation in the first place.

It's a peculiar paradox. To know how to win, you must win frequently. As Aristotle said, 'We are what we repeatedly do. Excellence then is not an act, but a habit'. You cannot be lackadaisical all your life and suddenly seek discipline in the middle of a big innings or before a big game. If you are a company that has always cut costs you cannot suddenly decide to become a big advertising spender. If you have grown up in a family with few means at its disposal, you will still eat the last corner slice of bread or vigorously shake the bottle of ketchup to extract the last drop even if you can easily afford another one. If you are a family-driven company, you cannot suddenly become a professionally-managed company, as Kumaramangalam Birla discovered when, as a young man, he took over the companies his charismatic father Aditya Birla had managed.

Winners Take Away Hope from the Opposition

Teams that win and win consistently, begin acquiring an aura around them. People write about them, opponents read that and watch in awe and when the time comes to compete, their rivals lack the self-belief so vital to a good contest. Losing becomes a self-fulfilling prophecy. This is one of the great truths in sport and that is why a lot of matches are won and lost before the match begins. Great teams are aware of this and that is why Australia's stated objective before the World Cup of 2003 was to create awe in the opposing dressing room. It meant that Australia would play and produce results in a manner that would allow them to focus on their game, while forcing their opponents to concentrate not on their own game as they should, but instead on Australia.

Similar instances have taken place in the past. When the West Indies were virtually invincible through the late seventies and mid-eighties, opponents would look at a line-up that read Greenidge, Haynes, Richards, Richardson, Gomes, Lloyd, Dujon, Marshall, Roberts, Holding and Garner. It created a sense of hopelessness in them and opposing teams have often spoken of losing matches before they had started. It's an interesting phenomenon this—creating hopelessness. The strongest weapon a team has on the field is hope. Till such time as hope is alive, they believe that they can win. Once hope dies, the end is swift. Steve Waugh, who was part of Australian teams that lost to the West Indies, often spoke of the desire to reach a similar level, where his team could win matches before they even began. Can organisations, like the West Indies cricket team, or indeed the great Bombay Ranji Trophy teams, kill hope before a contest starts? In her Harry Potter series, J. K. Rowling writes about the prison at Azkaban where soulless creatures called Dementors suck hope and happiness from the prisoners. These aren't torture chambers, no Guantanamo Bay here, they merely suck hope and that is why Azkaban was such a terrifying place.

It is an interesting exercise for organisations to carry out. Does your team have hope? Even on an off-day, or after a poor quarter, does the team believe it can win? If the opposite is true, the leader has a job to do, which is not necessarily to win the game, but it is to instill belief in his team, belief that could lead to a win.

This 'hopelessness' was vividly demonstrated before the semi-final of the Ranji Trophy in April 1991. The evening before the match, in the course of an informal discussion, it was suggested that Hyderabad had a chance against mighty Bombay, as they were then called. One of the players seemed to disagree. 'Nonsense,' he said (and here we are attempting a translation from the more colourful Hyderabadi dialect) 'if you get the openers out, Manjrekar walks in, if you get him out, Tendulkar comes in, then Vengsarkar, then Kambli, then Pandit, how many do you think we can dismiss?' Bombay batted the next day and went on to declare at 855-6 scored at just under 5 an over. A match had been lost even before it had begun and the action on the field was merely a self-fulfilling prophecy at work. Indeed at one stage when the Hyderabad captain pulled up a fielder for letting a boundary go through, he was told, 'What difference does four runs make when they have made seven hundred!'

To create this sense of hopelessness in the opposition, the Australians decided they would seek to win, not only every Test, but also every day and every session. When the opposition analysed a game, and broke it down session by session, they had to come to the conclusion that they had won very little, if indeed they had won anything at all. To drive home the point, the Aussies made a chart with the days on one axis and sessions on the other. It meant you had fifteen boxes and you ticked a box if you won, put a cross if you lost and an equal sign if the session was squared. Having done so, and discovered that their opponents had very little to show, they actually put the sign outside the dressing room, not inside, so that it could be seen by everyone! While that might have been rubbing it in a bit, the idea behind it was sound. If you want to create an aura you do not allow the opposition to believe they have a chance. If they win a session, they might start believing they could win a day and thereafter a game. They could enter a contest armed with hope and belief. So it was paramount that every session was conquered for the opposition to feel totally devoid of hope.

Nitin Paranjpe offers an interesting parallel from the world of consumer marketing. 'We have broken down our market into 153 cells,' he says 'and each cell is looked at independently. We might be winning overall but if even 25 of those cells are in red, it is not acceptable. And so while achieving the macro target is the desired outcome, the management of the business has to be more granular.'[5] In effect, HUL aim to win every session, every day, not just every match.

The hopelessness that such domination can generate can be seen through statements the opposition make. After another one-sided Ranji Trophy final, the captain of the losing side said, 'It was a privilege for us to play against Sachin Tendulkar,' much in the manner of India's bowlers who were in love with the idea of merely bowling to Don Bradman on their first tour there in 1948. If you are excited just by being on the same stage, chances are you are unlikely to out-perform the opposition.

Winning Teams Execute Plans to Perfection

Teams like these, that can dominate, are often excellent at converting their plans into action. They do the small things better than the opposition can, or wants to. It is incredible how many matches are won by teams that do the simple things, the one per cent things, better. In cricket that means working hard on fitness, running well between wickets, converting the opposition's three runs into two and your own two runs into three, taking catches, throwing at the stumps directly ... essentially things that do not require an extraordinary level of playing skill, but which can be learnt by consistent practice. These are teams that can do the difficult things very well, batting on bad pitches, bowling wicked out-swingers, turning the ball twelve inches on a flat surface, but assign just as much importance to the one per cent things. It is these one per cent things that produce consistency and you will find that across all areas of industry. Organisations that are consistently successful have strong systems and a framework to enforce those systems. In the course of our corporate sessions we often ask people, and the larger teams they represent, what their one per cent things are and how much time they spend practicing working on them. Doing the one per cent things is a sign of humility, while on the other hand ignoring them would be a mark of arrogance. It is also a great indicator of work ethic, the one factor more than any other that contributes to winning consistently.

> I fear not the man who practiced 10,000 kicks once. I fear the man who practiced one kick 10,000 times.
>
> —Bruce Lee

'The one per cent things tend to be stuff that is not particularly sexy,' says Niall Booker, former CEO of HSBC in India, 'and while it's tough to make an improvement of 25 per cent, it's possible to do 25 one-per-centers. In financial services, things like the industrialization of processes, control over data security, the handling of customer complaints and the protocols around the development of talent are the one per cent components. In banking, it could be risk management but more generally, these could be small details like sending thank-you notes to people who have done a good job, sharing a joke with your staff or addressing complaints of your smallest clients and showing them that you care—things that not everybody takes the time to do.'[6]

Mukul Deoras, then MD of Colgate-Palmolive (India) Ltd thinks the one per cent is alignment. 'It's not enough to have strategy. Execution is more important and in order to execute, the most important thing is alignment.'[7] Neeraj Garg, COO, Truecare Business, Abbott Truecare Pharma Pvt. Ltd echoes Mukul's views. 'Sometimes marketing programmes are planned and announced in a big way but marketing collaterals don't reach locations on time. Our different teams plan wonderfully in isolation but the field force that has to execute all this is overloaded because no one has looked at the programmes from their point of view.' [8] You may have thought through 'the big idea' thoroughly, but by overlooking the crucial one per cent you could prevent the idea from being fully effective.

Very often, young cricketers discover that what worked at one level may not work at another. For instance, while playing the Ranji Trophy they get used to receiving a bad ball every couple of overs which they can put away. However, at the international level, they may have to wait an hour, and so acquiring patience and the ability to pick the right ball to hit becomes critical. The style which worked at the first-class level may no longer produce long innings for them, and so they will need to up their game. The same goes with young bowlers who can sometimes expect to get away with a bad ball in domestic cricket. However at the international level, they realize that they will be hammered if they don't maintain line and length discipline. Higher levels of competition demand higher levels of execution.

When the contest is close, there is no scope for error and as Nitin Paranjpe puts it, 'even a momentary lapse in attention can lead to disproportionate damage'. Vishwanathan Anand experienced this first-hand in his famous match against Magnus Carlsen in Chennai. In an interview post the match Anand said that Carlsen got the better of him because of his ability to stay focused over longer periods. Anand faltered in the fifth game, never to recover in that match.

Over the years many players have won at Wimbledon. They were all good but the names that come to mind when we say champions are Becker, Federer, Djokovic ... players who have won time and again. Consistency creates the aura that surrounds champions. In business, consistency comes from top class execution. The Domino's promise of delivery in 30 minutes flat would fail if they couldn't deliver during the monsoon. Customer service needs to meet standards irrespective of the location of the consumer and Indigo or Jet Airways have to keep a tight control on their flight schedules if they need to top the rankings.

Run outs and dropped catches are classic examples of poor execution. While communication between players could be a factor, more often than not it's the lack of clarity in roles that results in a casualty. Not knowing who should go after the ball leads to lack of ownership and poor accountability. Holding on to the ball for longer than necessary and passing to the wrong player will have parallels in every kind of business.

Agility has become really critical in an uncertain world. 'Planning cycles have gone down and goals are less hard-coded', says Saugata Gupta.[9] 'It's about speed and excellence … it's an "and" and not an "or". It's about getting it right fastest. And if you go wrong, then about correcting it quickly', he adds making it sound like a T20 match. The high-speed short format game has had a lasting effect on the way the one-day games are played. 'In many cases, agility is a bigger strength than ability', thinks D. Shivakumar, strengthening Saugata's view.[10]

At the 2003 Cricket World Cup in South Africa, a number of the Pakistani players were focussed on individual records and there was no mention of a collective desire to win the event. In order to win a game however, you need everyone in the team to pull together. The team has to work as a unit. However, the Pakistan team, though immensely talented, lacked this collective effort, and the result is known to all. On the contrary, in 2005, an All-Stars World XI was created to beat Australia. Alas! With no time to gel and with little in common to bond them together, the All-Stars were no match for the well-oiled juggernaut, losing by huge margins amidst a media frenzy.

A hallmark of a good team is that it is capable of winning in all playing conditions. As a large number of cricketers play all three formats of the game, they need to switch from one to the other in their play as well as in their mind. Marathon runners need to adapt to diverse terrain, varying altitudes and different climatic conditions. Grand Slam winners too show their skill in being able to adapt their game to each surface and that's what makes them special.

After Monty Panesar made his test debut in 2006 against India, he showed great promise. Two-and-a half years later, he hadn't managed to bring too much variation into his bowling. He became predictable, and batsmen could read him with ease. And so one day, in his typically no-nonsense style, Shane Warne asked during commentary, 'Is Monty playing his thirty-third test, or is he playing his first test for the thirty-third time?' If you don't innovate, you become predictable. Innovation helps in delighting the customer and stealing a march over your competition at least till the time they catch up. Innovation has become the mantra in the age of start-ups and disruption. Most people associate innovation with strategy or business models but Ronnie Screwvala very rightly says, 'Innovation is as much in execution as it is in ideation.'[11]

Execution is about honing your skill through practice but a skill is not much use if you cannot summon it when you need it the most. That's why many curses in the Mahabharata revolve round characters who are blessed with extraordinary powers that fail them at a time when they are most needed! Even the best teams know what it is to falter under pressure; the South African cricketers being the ones most familiar with this feeling. In sport, we often talk about 'big occasion' players who can hold their nerve when pressure and scrutiny are at their highest. While there are many players who are like bone china crockery—very pretty but of delicate disposition, champions are like tough coffee mugs or the south Indian tumbler—not necessarily stylish but someone you can trust to deliver.

Charged up teams with a mission are excited about delivering and do deliver at most times. The challenge comes when business is going through a dull phase and people are not at their sharpest best. It is up to the leader then to keep the team hungry and motivated. Imran Khan, it is said had the ability to stay hawk-eyed and focussed even in boring test matches heading towards a draw. He never let the intensity drop for himself as well as his team. Joy Bhattacharya who spent a crucial few years in helping build the Kolkata Knight Riders team says that their coach Dav Whatmore used to call KKR 'the team that runs even between overs.' Even when bowlers got hammered for many runs, they need to see a positive and energetic side supporting them. Companies with large workforces of young and restless Gen-Yers who need constant challenges need to be particularly careful to see that employees are constantly motivated and don't get bored.

Newsweek magazine once did a great cover story on Tiger Woods and how he dominated his sport. But the biggest revelation about the article was what other leading sportspersons had to say. In that story, Joe Montana, a US pro-football legend said, 'He gets on a roll, and everybody else starts looking at the board to see what Tiger is doing. They are watching TV too, and they should be playing.' That is what champions do. They force you to divert attention from your game to theirs. You don't look at your strengths, you look at theirs! Sometimes you can see this feeling of awe in our markets as well. It used to be said about HUL, that in their heyday, when they introduced a new product in the market they made life virtually impossible for the opposition. Anindo Mukherjee, earlier Managing Director, General Mills India, (and formerly with HUL) told us, 'In the mid-eighties, HUL developed a unique technology for soap-making that gave them a huge cost advantage over competitors. Consequently, over the next decade, it became very difficult for other players in this category to compete with them. Several of them fell by the wayside including large, established companies like TOMCO, which was ultimately acquired by HUL. Over this period, HUL's market share rose from the mid-forties to mid-seventies. For competitors, it was a hopeless, futile fight.'[12]

Later we were to see something similar with Reliance, a company that intimidated people with the sheer magnitude of their imagination and the ability to convert that into reality. It is a powerful thought and should serve as an inspiration to champions. Ask yourself, can you win a match before it begins?

The Look of a Winner

Inevitably then, champions make their intentions known in the manner in which they carry themselves. The key question to ask yourself about a player, or indeed a speaker or a sales executive is, does he look like he wants to be there? Or does he look like he would rather be elsewhere? When you saw Viv Richards taking the field, you could almost sense the intensity. The swagger as he walked, eyes a bit bloodshot, a few pearls of sweat. He looked more like a heavyweight boxer entering the ring and everything about his body language said, 'Right, I'm here; let's see if you can get me.'

Body language is critical in sport as it is in everything we do, because the way we carry ourselves tells the person in front of us what we think about ourselves. As you walk into a situation, your self-image walks along with you as well. You can carry a swagger, you can put on an act for a while but in the end your inner confidence or lack of it always reveals itself. Dean Jones told us this great story about playing against the West Indies in their glory days. He was a young man and very nervous but was trying to mask it by putting on a brave front. While he was batting, Desmond Haynes at short leg kept laughing. 'What are you laughing about?' Jones asked. 'You're scared, aren't you?' Haynes said. Jones thought he would be a bit smart and said, 'Yeah, but don't tell Joel (Garner).' To which Haynes responded with more laughter. 'What now?' Jones asked. Haynes paused for a moment and replied, 'He already knows,' and broke into more peals of laughter.

Geoffrey Boycott, for example, liked to walk out to bat as soon as the opposition had walked out, to convey to them that he was ready for them, that he was waiting to take them on. Sunil Gavaskar used to get very upset if the two openers didn't walk out together because he thought they were conveying a message to the opposition. Famously, in a Test in the West Indies, when he was hit on the side of the head, he did not even touch the spot—he didn't want the bowler to know that he was hurt. Mohinder Amarnath who was batting at the other end, said he feared for Gavaskar when he heard the sound of the ball hitting him but was amazed when Gavaskar simply stretched himself and got ready for the next delivery. At the end of the over when the substitute, Kiran More, charged out with a glass of water asking if he needed help, he got an earful from Gavaskar. He didn't want to give the bowlers an inch, didn't want to let them know they had scored a point.(When we spoke to Ajinkya Rahane for this book and asked him if there was a bowler who troubled him, he didn't want to say so on tape. He didn't want the bowler, if he ever saw it, to believe he had scored a point!)

Even Tendulkar, known for his great equanimity, has been known to make a point through his body language. 'In my case there have been occasions when the bowlers have said a lot of things and I have not reacted at all. And sometimes I have started it, when I felt that if I do something the bowler might get disturbed and do something else. You don't always need to say something, it might just be looking a bowler in the eye because when you do that the bowler knows you mean business.'

Organisations have a certain body language as well. For example, Reliance is big, brash, and its scale of operations is mind-boggling; the Tatas are firm, understated, classy; Infosys is honest and open. It is a good exercise to carry out. Anil Ambani's entertainment venture is called Reliance Big; Infosys came clean when one of their senior managers was accused of sexual harassment; Ratan Tata put his cards on the table and bid goodbye to Singur at some cost to his Nano project. You don't expect Mukesh Ambani to think small either and his ambition of building the world's largest refinery has not surprised anyone.

Probably body language is best manifest in the area of sales where the retailer knows that the salesperson requires the sale to achieve his targets, and yet the salesperson needs to appear committed enough to convince the retailer that it is in his interest to place an order. Sometimes the salesperson needs to sell a couple of extras to the retailer; or the product manager has to appear more convinced than he really is to the advertising agency. It is a game that is critical for success. It is a game that must be played well, not an act that is lightly worn for it can expose people.

Here are some questions every organisation must look at very closely. How do their employees appear to the outside world? What is the message they are subliminally conveying about themselves and their company?

The Winner's Mind

For all their ruthlessness, sportsmen, and indeed all winners need to have the demeanour of a monk. Sport is about calm minds and violent bodies, the reverse rarely works. It is difficult to stay calm amidst the pressure to perform. Abhinav Bindra, India's gold medalist in shooting at the 2008 Beijing Olympics, actually practiced it through an unusual combination.

'Essentially, it was adrenaline training—rope-climbing, scaling walls, walking on a tightrope 70 or 80 feet above the ground. The idea is to get a rush, a flow of adrenaline, and then to remain calm in that situation.'[13]

'A calm mind is not about doing nothing', says Ajinkya Rahane. 'It's about keeping yourself busy, particularly if you are going through a tough phase. It prevents your mind from being flooded with negative thoughts.'[14] Rahane found that 'switching off' after about fifteen minutes of introspection post a match made him more relaxed; very important for someone as intense and analytical as him.

Buddhist monks frequently talk about living in the present and ridding the mind of the baggage of the past and the anxiety of the future. Like individual sportsmen, teams tend to carry their baggage with them as well. Teams that have had glorious pasts, like the Indian hockey squad or the Mumbai Ranji Trophy side, can sometimes run the risk of living in the past. We recently met the head of a leading advertising agency who said his company's showreel still began with advertising created in the early Eighties. For years, Mumbai cricketers used to talk of their 'glorious heritage' and of how it was easier to play for India than it was to play for Mumbai. Indian coaches, locked in the past, focussed on dribbling skills unaware that hockey had long transformed into a game of speed and power. Sometimes a great past can make teams oblivious to the present and force them to live in denial. England kept talking about test cricket when there was a revolution taking place in limited overs cricket.

It can frustrate the modern player since he is constantly being compared to legendary figures from the past. A sportsperson succinctly summed it for us when he remarked that players seem to get better every day after they retire. Teams need to build on their heritage not get blinded by it and maybe the best way to do that is to embrace the present and address the needs of the present. In fact, Viren Rasquinha, former captain of the

Indian hockey team said he couldn't relate to some of his coaches because they talked about players and styles he had never seen.

It is critical that the team on the field is given the impression that it is the lineup of the day; that it is the team that is going to deliver. It must be empowered. Glorifying players who have retired or are unavailable at the expense of current-day players demeans those who are actually playing.

Some other teams might have had a very ordinary past and can carry wounds of defeat. Since the only thing they are good at is losing, they tend to lapse into a cycle of defeat from time to time; often they hold back, taking tentative steps when a giant stride might make a difference. Teams that are locked into the past need fresh leadership and newer players who have not yet been painted by the brush of defeat. South Africa did that when they picked a brash 22-year-old to be their cricket captain. Graeme Smith had played very little international cricket and was clearly ambitious but his biggest qualification was that he had never played with or under the charismatic, and later disgraced, Hansie Cronje. South Africa needed to turn over a new leaf, break its links with a past that was overwhelming and negative. Initially, there was a great deal of turmoil and pain but it turned out to be an excellent decision. The Indian team that toured Pakistan on that path-breaking tour of 2004 had only one player (Tendulkar when he was 16!) who had played there and so were free of the fear of losing in Pakistan.

Good teams are able to leave this baggage behind when they take the field but equally, they are able to put aside the anxiety of the future. Mukul Deoras shares one of the rules that his company followed during the launch of a new product which already had a powerful competitor. 'Be nimble and flexible, to change resources but never lose hope,' he says, and most importantly, do not demoralize the team, don't make the competitor into an invincible demon.' Sanjay Manjrekar told us of how one of his coaches asked him to read about how one of his opponents became a great bowler. 'I was going to bat against him the next day and my coach was telling me how great the bowler was. I couldn't believe it.'

Winners visualize the rewards of success, losers visualize the penalties of failure.

When asked about why an outstanding Pakistan team lost the final of the 1999 World Cup rather tamely, their captain at the time, the great Wasim Akram, said too many people were worried about what would have happened if they lost. Rather than thinking of winning, they were consumed by the fear of a possible reaction to defeat. It is a telling insight.

Perhaps top sportsmen and teams, top executives and corporations, can learn from those Buddhist monks who have a wonderful way of being at peace and living in the present. Former English cricketer and brilliant coach Bob Woolmer, who died suddenly during the 2007 World Cup, often used to quote Joan Rivers, 'Yesterday is history, tomorrow is a mystery.' Good teams win, move on and get ready for the next day.

Hallmarks of Winning Teams

- Band of boys atmosphere, happy and relaxed.

- Ability to pass the ball.

- Living in the present, planning for the future.

- Carrying everyone along—backing up under-performers.

- A 'can-do' approach.

- Being attentive to the one per cent things.

- Common shared vision.

- Strong personal goals yet subordinate to team goals.

- Focussing on competition, not internal differences.

- Non-negotiable work ethic.

- Bringing in new people and ideas to prevent staleness.

- Nurturing or culling at the right moment.

- Hunger, passion, energy.

Goals

There's nothing wrong with having your goals really high and trying to achieve them. That's the fun part. You may come up short. I've come up short on a lot on my goals, but it's always fun to try and achieve them.

—Tiger Woods

There are certain things in life that you want to accomplish or milestones that you may wish to achieve. Fix a deadline and just go ahead and do them. Then there are others, those wonderful feel- good things that you always wanted to do, which you store away at the back of your mind for retrieval when you really have the time for them. Occasionally, these thoughts will surface to become interesting topics of conversation and retreat to the inner recesses of your mind soon after. The first set of thoughts or ideas are your goals, the second, your dreams.

The moment you put a deadline on your dream, it becomes a goal. Sometimes a dream doesn't remain as attractive as it did when it was first stored snugly in your head.

You are accountable for your goals, but not for your dreams and maybe it is the fear of being accountable that keeps some things in the realm of dreamland. For example, thinking that 'I am going to learn how to bowl the slower ball' or 'I am going to send in this beautiful cross from the left' or 'I am going to clean up the house' will remain dreams unless you decide by when you are going to achieve them. There have been many young batsmen who have probably told themselves that they would learn to play the short ball and of course never did; similarly there are many young executives whose to-do list has remained the same on the first of every month.

Goals Must Be Out of Reach But Not Out of Sight

So what kind of goals should we set for ourselves so that they are transferred from the realm of fantasy and begin to nudge the real world with a deadline? Perhaps goals that are not too high, since that could mean that they will always remain dreams, but not so low either that achieving them presents no challenge. The classic line of course, and a great line as well, is that goals should be slightly out of reach but never out of sight. One person who did that extraordinarily well all his life was Rahul Dravid, who combined work ethic with great ability. He believes it is always better to set challenging goals even if that means occasionally falling slightly short, rather than set simple goals which could lead to dissatisfaction and leave you wondering if they were too easy. Often people are inclined to set rather simple goals for themselves, and in the process they forget that the kind of goals one sets tells the world what kind of person you are. This is perhaps best highlighted in *Harry Potter and the Chamber of Secrets* when Dumbledore tells the young Harry Potter, 'It is our choices, Harry, that show what we truly are, far more than our abilities.' This applies to young students, sales executives, opening batsmen and leaders of giant corporations equally.

Dravid, like Anil Kumble, is a great example of someone who became as good as he could be. He did that through a process of setting goals and working diligently towards achieving them. Dravid says that at various points in time he has set performance as well as result goals for himself, but believes that performance goals work better for him because the result is not always in his control. 'Even if I set a result goal of scoring a century I could get out to a bad decision or a really good ball or maybe score 95, which still means I haven't reached my goal. Performance goals are far more realistic, achievable and often take the stress out of the result. Besides, if you consistently achieve performance goals, you invariably end up achieving your result goal.' In 1997-98 as he was struggling to find gaps in the field against Kenya and Bangladesh, it seemed he would never be able to become a quality one-day player. Within five years Dravid was India's best finisher, not just the sheet anchor laying the stage for the others but the finisher in limited-overs cricket. In effect when he says it is better to set higher goals, he is talking of what the corporate world calls stretch goals; goals that cause you to dig deeper, extract just that little bit more out of yourself; cause you to liberate yourself from the comfort zone you are happily ensconced in.

One of the things we do when we have slightly longer sessions with corporate teams is either to analyse case studies or, sometimes, to play a little game like this one: we divide the people into two teams and ask one team to run towards pre-determined spots where a set of tennis balls are kept. Each runner has to reach the spot, pick up the ball, throw it to the person collecting it and run towards the next one and so on. There are a couple of rules, one of which is that you cannot throw a ball unless the earlier one has been collected and placed in a basket. The opposing team is allowed to distract you by directing you towards the wrong spot, which can become confusing because it takes time to figure out the order in which you have to run. In one of our sessions we had set 45 seconds as the time in which to carry out the entire sequence of running towards a ball, throwing it to the gatherer, running to the next spot and repeating this exercise over five spots. The first time the sales executives did it, they took between 43 and 47 seconds. We then reset the target to 35 seconds and discovered, maybe because of the learning curve, that most teams could get there as well. At which point, the managing director of the company threw them a challenge. 'Let's show them we can do it in 25,' he said and we discovered to our great joy that while nobody could hit 25 seconds, many of them were no more than a couple of seconds away. It was a very simple yet practical demonstration of what Dravid was talking about, that if you set your goals high, you may not always achieve them but you are likely to do much better than when you set small, easily achievable goals. In the session that afternoon, the idea of setting stretch goals went through quite easily.

You Never Know How Good You Can Be

There is another school of thought finding acceptance in corporate India. It's got an interesting title, though one of the words is a bit difficult to fathom. Set BHAG goals, some people are saying. Big Hairy Audacious Goals. The origin lies in the thought that we often don't know how good we are and that sometimes it is good to embark on a journey into the unfamiliar.

Neeraj Garg has an interesting, though slightly different, point of view on this. 'Initially the goal may sound crazy, even unachievable. Then, once you do it, the self-belief is unbelievable. When I was an Area Sales Manager in Karnataka with Hindustan Lever, selling Brooke Bond Red Label Tea, the weekly turnover in a market was 30 tonnes. I announced a week where we would aim to touch 100 tonnes. All our resources were pooled and the target was achieved. This created a "can do" feeling in the team. The subsequent months showed sales settling down at a level lower than 100 but much higher than 30. What you achieve is a function of what you think you can.'[1]

Nitin Paranjpe, then at HUL, tells an interesting story going back to 2009 when they realised that distribution had traditionally been their strength and while they were still ahead, competitors had slowly begun to narrow the gap. 'The context of that was we were distributing to about a million outlets and adding about ten thousand new outlets every year. We had added about fifty thousand outlets over five years and we asked ourselves what could we do which is truly discontinuous. It might sound outlandish when I mention it, but we started off with a number, which was 500,000. Of course, there was a theoretical construct—outlets existed, we were not creating them,' recalled Nitin.[2] Interestingly, not only did they achieve the planned 500,000 but actually went on to do 600,000! The additional learning, he said was that there wasn't any negotiation, five hundred is as silly as ridiculous as four hundred thousand. So, this whole act of trying to talk down a target (so normal in any discussion on targets!) because you are afraid, you will fail ... disappears.

Sometimes it requires a pioneer to set such an audacious goal. Once it has been achieved, It opens the minds of others and they attack it armed with the belief that it is possible. That is often the clincher. Belief. Once Roger Bannister went past the mile in under four minutes, others quickly followed suit. A double century in a one-day international was inconceivable, why there was an era where a century was considered a distant landmark. Once Sachin Tendulkar got it in 2010, many more were scored. And now, the idea that someone will match Sachin Tendulkar's hundred international centuries seems inconceivable too. But who knows, someone might get there one day.

Audacious goals aren't for the faint-hearted or for the sceptics, of whom every team has a fair representation, because as we will see shortly, they can strangle teams, create fear and lead to a loss in confidence. For most teams a goal slightly out of reach is the more easily attainable.

Sadly, we do not always know what the ideal stretch goals for us are because it is a very rare person who knows how good he or she can be. Imran Khan, one of the all-time greats of the game and an outstanding leader, often talks of how he tried to be the best fast bowler from Pakistan. When he set the goal, he was very far away from achieving it, he was in fact just another privileged eighteen-year-old whose ego had been bruised by the real world that so many of us are usually sheltered from. Imran did eventually get there, through a process of understanding his action and remodelling it. He wouldn't have gone through the danger of doing that if he didn't have a clear goal in sight; a goal that he believed was slightly out of reach but never out of sight. To others, maybe, but not to him. Then he set himself the goal of becoming the finest fast bowler in the world, which in the eyes of many, he briefly ascended to, most dramatically during the 1982-83 series against India when he took 41 wickets and produced several spells where he seemed unplayable. Thereafter his goal was to be the best captain Pakistan has had. Which he undeniably became!

This assessment of how good you are, or indeed can be, is critical. Imran talks about recognising your limitations and then working steadfastly towards expanding the range you can work in. It is an interesting thought. You first accept what you are capable of, which means you know how good you can be at that stage then work towards rejecting those limitations. It's like saying, 'I accept that my current skills will not allow me to be the financial analyst I want to be so I will work towards erasing those limitations and then become the financial analyst I want to be.'

It is just as true though that a vast majority of people either over-estimate their ability or sell themselves short. Hence the importance of what Imran is saying, of knowing how good you are and accepting the situation before setting out to change it.

Two cricketers who were excellent at this were the Australian captain, Steve Waugh, and the champion Indian leg spinner, Anil Kumble. Neither of them was possessed of the kind of glittering talent that a Brian Lara or a Shane Warne had, but Waugh and Kumble constantly raised the bar on their performance themselves. Waugh in fact called his book *Out of My Comfort Zone* and Kumble memorably said, 'All his life Sachin Tendulkar had to live up to people's expectations, I had to change them!' Both set themselves very high personal performance goals and had no time for mediocrity, whether in their own cricket or anyone else's. They proved that a combination of work ethic and challenging goals could lead you to achieve anything.

When we asked Sachin Tendulkar how difficult it was to live up to the expectations of a billion people, he said he judges his performance by his own standards and not by what people expect of him. So while the nation went into raptures over his double hundred in a one-dayer against South Africa in 2010 he didn't think it was that special for him personally. While he was happy that he could do it at the age of 36 against one of the top sides in the world, he felt that on a good day if someone had 50 overs to bat, 200 was achievable. For Sachin, a far more commendable record was when he got to 35 Test centuries and 10,000 runs something that was personally far more exciting and in his own words 'the ultimate challenge'. And now of course, he has laid down the challenge for the next generation to get a hundred international centuries! Maybe in a much later version of this book, or one that someone else will write, a player will talk of the challenge of getting there!

Apart from audacious goals being set and then being achieved, the timeframes for achieving goals have collapsed dramatically. A decade ago someone had mentioned to us that it took about seventeen years to become a partner in a Big Four accounting firm. Now we find people in their thirties becoming CEOs. Don't be surprised if a player gets to break Sachin's formidable record earlier than you think!

Goals Can Overwhelm

As we said a little while ago, one of the reasons people are loath to stretch themselves, is the overwhelming fear of failure. In India for some reason, we look down upon failure, we regard it as irreversible, we push those who fail into a corner, treat them like outcasts. Wasim Akram, one of Pakistan's finest fast bowlers says, 'In our part of the world, if you don't win consistently, you get flak from the press or from your own people but in the west they just say bad luck, tomorrow is another day. We need to learn that.' Hence, the tendency to play safe at most times. Ravi Shastri and Virender Sehwag are two other cricketers, who, despite their contrasting playing styles, showed the power of stretching. Shastri found that every time the going got tough, he was being asked to open the batting, but his approach was, 'If I can score when others are struggling, I show my class,' and so he took up opening the innings as a challenge and did extremely well in that position. So too with Sehwag who, after a brilliant century on debut when he batted at number six, was asked by Sourav Ganguly to open in England. At first, he was hesitant, but took up the challenge and became one of the most destructive players in cricketing history in that position. On either occasion, if the player had worried about what happened if he failed, he would never have taken up the challenge. It is a great lesson for all of us. Who knows how many opportunities we might have missed out on, simply because we looked at them in anticipation of failure.

However, when stretch goals are set too high they can strangle you because they may appear too large, too unattainable, too far away; quite like the feeling you may get looking up at Mount Everest when you haven't yet reached base camp one. A number of pharma MNCs reported that with the changing patent laws all eyes were on India, both as a large domestic market and as a manufacturing base. Sales targets that were set for the Indian teams left them overwhelmed and skeptical. Nobody really sets out to climb Everest or chase 350 runs in a one-day game because one runs the risk of achieving something substantial and is yet weighed down by all that is still left to do. The best players break down their large goals into smaller ones that seem attainable. In doing so, they are never really chasing the large goal, only the smaller portion.

This could be an issue for people with large but long-term goals. People who work on infrastructure projects, for example. Or shooters for whom the big event, the Olympics comes once every four years. Abhinav Bindra told us that his training academy in the US where he spent six years had a motto which said: 'It's not every four years, it is every day.'[3] And so every day, he set himself small goals that required some degree of effort but were achievable goals. Those are important, he says since all your happiness cannot be tied to that single, huge goal which finally may or may not happen. So, there is hope and fulfillment on the way, the satisfaction of having achieved something and the inspiration to achieve the next goal.

Similarly, the mountaineer attempting to scale Everest aims to reach base camp two and then base camp three. A team chasing 350 seeks to score 100 for the loss of no more than one wicket in the first 15 overs, then maybe 50 in the next ten. The challenge on Everest will begin on the last leg, while in the run chase for 350 it will only begin when no more than 80 or 100 runs are left. The challenge for the Premiership in English football for example, begins as a goal at the start of the season and is reflected in the kind of players picked, the quality of replacements and other such factors. The immediate goal is always to win the next game, or if the team is set back by injuries, not to drop too many points in the week. The hunt for the title, as an immediate goal, begins only in the last six weeks.

Therefore you need to break down the long term goals into a series of achievable short-term goals. Having purely short-term goals without a larger objective can cause teams to take short cuts, to 'just get it done with,' to do something that might end up hurting them, and in some cases even do something they might regret later. Breaking down goals into short-term achievables allows you to cater to the immediate without losing focus on where you are headed.

In 1976, India was set a target of 403 by the West Indies to win the third Test. Only one team in the history of the game had scored more than 400 to win a game and India weren't the best batting side in the world either.

They surprised everybody by scoring 406 for four. A few years later when he was asked what the strategy was, Sunil Gavaskar said the plan was to just keep batting session by session; at the start of a session to take care not to get out, then tell yourself you had done the difficult part and would be foolish to throw it away and towards the end to ensure you were around at the start of the next. The assault on 403 only began much, much later.

A good sales executive knows what we are talking about. When he is given the target for the following year, he can easily throw in the towel. He knows that if he breaks it down into quarterly, monthly even weekly targets, it doesn't seem very daunting. He can keep patting himself on the back for small goals achieved and stay positive about hitting the larger, more distant one. In effect, he ends up making the larger goal a by-product of executing precisely defined small goals very well. The larger goal happens!

At Hobart in 2012, India were set a stiff target of 321 by Sri Lanka in a one-day international. Unfortunately, to go ahead on net run rate, India had to get those runs in 40 overs or less. A young Virat Kohli gave an early glimpse into why he eats targets for dinner scoring 133 in 86 balls and finishing off the target in 36.4 overs. When asked afterwards how he planned the chase he said that they often had to chase 160 in a T20 game to win and so he worked out that two T20 chases back-to-back would do the trick. As it turns out, at the twenty-over mark, India were exactly 160-2! Getting there was dramatic enough, but the idea behind how to approach a difficult target was even more inspiring.

Sometimes even the immediate goal can appear daunting and teams or even individuals can run the risk of giving up before the effort begins. At such times, it helps to present the goal in a manner that suggests it is achievable. It doesn't change the goal, instead it merely restates it in a manner that appears less daunting and provides the resolve to go after it. When, for example, Australia had made a world record 434 for four against South Africa in 2006, the immediate reaction would have been to sit in the dressing room with drooping heads and hope that the day would end quickly and South African players wouldn't look like fools. Instead, one of the senior players, Jacques Kallis, suggested that given the weather and the pitch conditions a score of about 450 was par and that Australia were probably 15 runs short. It broke the ice, cleared the air of despondency in the dressing room and set the mood for a historic chase and subsequent win. The comment didn't win South Africa the game, it merely created the atmosphere in which the run chase could be mounted.

Or again, when India were set 360 to win the World Cup in 2003 against an outstanding Australian team that seemed to add a further 30 runs to the total by the way they caught, fielded and bowled. The dressing room in the break couldn't have been the happiest place to be in. Until Sachin asked a simple question of them: 'Can we score one boundary an over?' It's not easy but neither is it impossible. When he heard a few players say yes, he asked what the target would then reduce to ... a boundary an over means 50 balls produce 200 runs and the objective shrinks to 160 from 250 balls. Very achievable. Again it was the manner in which a seemingly impossible target was reframed that made it seem surmountable. It didn't change the target, or as it turned out, the result, but it put the team in the right frame of mind to tackle an overwhelming goal.

It's Not Always About Being Number One

Sometimes, small, precise, performance-related goals can produce extraordinary results. This is especially true of people who are already on the path to success and need that little something to improve their basket of offerings. The off-spinner might want to learn the *doosra* (the ball that goes away from the batsman), something that took Muralitharan's career into orbit; or the batsman might want to play the switch hit or the hook shot, a fielder might want to throw underarm with his left arm if he is right-handed. Often therefore your goals can be determined by where you have reached in your area of expertise; the beginner has larger goals, the expert has smaller, more clearly defined ones.

Normally when one thinks of winning, we visualise the number one position. This may not always be the case. Sunil Lulla, Chairman and Managing Director, Grey Group India, considers Marico a big winner since it stood up to a giant like Hindustan Unilever Limited and is considered a leader in innovation with brands like Parachute, Saffola and Kaya, each one a leader in its respective product category. 'You don't have to be number one, two or three any more. Even in advertising, there is place for niche, creative boutiques,' he says.[4]

Sometimes being no.1 may not even be an option. Niall Booker, who was an outstanding country head at HSBC in India and is an extremely erudite leader, says, 'It is important to set stretching, but attainable goals. It doesn't have to be about being number one. For example, I would set a goal for the quality of our service, our return on equity, cost income ratio and implementation of our corporate and social policy objectives. These goals might not make me the number one bank in each of these categories but the contribution of these put me in the space where I want to be. It is realistic for Tiger Woods to want to be the number one golfer in the world; it is not for me; but I can still aim to knock a stroke or two off my handicap.'[5]

Niall is absolutely right, for diverse teams at various achievement levels can set themselves different goals.

The Australian cricket team, for example, could set themselves the target of becoming number one and in course of time staying at that spot. However that would be an unrealistic target for, say, Bangladesh. In their early years while they were struggling, their coach Dav Whatmore, set an interesting goal for them. Rather than setting the objective of winning a game, which could lead to frustration and disillusionment, he told his batsmen that the goal was to bat out fifty overs against a strong attack. Doing that would be a battle won and would get the team to believe that the next goal was attainable.

Indeed, the definition of number one could be misleading. In the credit card industry, for example, profitability is perhaps a better goal to have than merely having the largest customer base. In telecom, companies might seek to have the highest revenue per subscriber rather than a larger but less profitable base. It is eventually about maximising the resources you can put behind an effort, which is why Booker said (and was seconded by the former England captain, Nasser Hussain) that he quite admired New Zealand as a cricketing nation. They have a very small player base and given that, they frequently over-achieve, often punching above their weight.

Stephen Fleming, their erudite former captain, says that given the small player base they learn very quickly to make the most of what they have to be competitive. It is something, he said, he was told as a child: make the most of what you have. Think about it and you realise why they are such respected competitors.

Performance Goals Versus Result Goals

That leads us to a very interesting debate about what kind of goals to set. Often we can get obsessed with results, for that is what guarantees our worth. Indeed, that is what we play for, or work for; that is what we hope will grant us our place in the sun, give us the best memories of our lives. Yet, this obsession with the result can become the biggest impediment towards achieving it. As we come closer or maybe encounter frustrating hurdles, we can get desperate; the calmness that is so important to performance could desert us. We see this in sport very often, as we did with South Africa. When teams are on the brink of major success, they suddenly get tense, are in a hurry to get to the result, panic and start doing things that are different from what brought them close to victory in the first place. Bowlers take eight wickets and suddenly look to bowl magic balls instead of continuing to bowl to their strengths and being patient. Teams play outstanding football for eighty minutes, lead by a goal and then suddenly decide they want to play out time. The defence gets overcrowded, there are panic clearances and inevitably, a goal is scored against them.

There is therefore great substance in the point of view that the easiest way to remove the anxiety associated with the result is to make it irrelevant, to ignore it, indeed not even to play for it but instead to merely let it happen. The objective of playing is to deliver peak performance, which is often in your control, rather than to produce a result where you rarely control all the variables. As

India's badminton champion Saina Nehwal puts it, 'I want to be 100 per cent at every tournament. I'm not concerned about rankings. If I win, my ranking will improve. My focus is on improving my game and fitness. If that happens, everything else follows.'[6]

So athletes should aim to deliver performance, the pursuit of which should lead to the result. For example, winning a gold medal at the Olympics can be a dream but you cannot control what the others are likely to do. The swimmer for example, rather than swim for gold swims for the timing, which is in his/her control and that is most likely to produce gold. A batsman rather than batting for a century says he will bat for three hours at the end of which he will most likely have got a hundred.

Setting performance goals therefore, not only takes away the anxiety of the result but allows you to come away aware of the fact that you gave your best. It's a philosophy shared by Viswanathan Anand, chess champion and (former) world number one. 'I just turn up at tournaments and play my chess and see what happens. With tournaments like Linares I think you play to the best of your abilities and see how everyone else performs. This was my attitude in 1998, so it's nothing new I've come up with. I don't see the point of speculating too much. I just like to play and see how things develop.'[7]

For the truth is that there is no shame in losing after having performed the best you can, provided of course you are honest enough to know that you did indeed deliver the best that you could. There is however much to feel small about if you haven't tried hard enough. For to lose is not a crime, to offer less than 100 per cent is.

Vivek Kudva, Managing Director, Franklin Templeton Investments, India and CEEMEA, believes that, 'Both performance goals and result goals are important. Without result goals, managers will not know what the end objective is. Without performance goals the end may become more important than the means and it may become more difficult to replicate success.'[8] The sporting parallel to that could well be that you think about the result goal before and after a match but focus on the performance goal during the game and in training.

'Actually, coaches calculate what level you need to achieve to win gold or silver, but then break it down into small increments or whatever and give that as a performance goal to the athlete. In business, we need to convert the result goal into small activities and steps that the sales person needs to do on a daily and weekly basis. It's easier for them to understand.' elaborates Neeraj Garg.[9] Performance goals though are not for the lazy and the disinclined, for those who set themselves easily attainable performance standards, sit back and claim that they have delivered a 100 per cent. That won't take you too far. It is a completely different argument about whether everyone needs to go far in life but then real satisfaction only comes from being as good as we can be.

The pharma sector in India has undergone a sea change and calculation of market size and market shares has become a pointless exercise. 'The Indian market is growing rapidly, and the nature of competition changing due to new entrants and mergers and acquisitions activity. In this context, market share by sales value alone can be a poor measure of performance. One should look at other metrics such as size of business, share of a specific segment of the market, or even share of a customer group (hospitals, consultant physicians, etc). One has to use a metric that can be read consistently so as to provide a true reflection of performance,' says Neeraj Garg.[10] He says that they would rather just set sales and growth targets for Nicholas Piramal.

In addition to the normal target-driven players, there are others that play a supporting role, but without whom the attainment of the goal of peak performance would be almost impossible. HR managers, for example, in an increasingly stressful world, create a work environment that encourages performance. Trainers work on athletes to keep their bodies ready for peak performance. If we only assigned result goals, how would we assess their contribution? Setting performance goals allows them to be assessed for the specific role they play.

Steve Waugh in his excellent book on the World Cup campaign of 1999, *No Regrets-A Captain's Diary*, writes that he told his team that it would be a 'no regrets tour'; that irrespective of the result, his team would leave England with their heads held high. 'Once in England, I introduced a new title—The No Regrets Tour—which reflected what I wanted from myself and all involved. Nothing left to luck, no "what ifs" or "if onlys", simply a concerted, full-on team effort that would maximise our chances of victory.' Not a single player, he said, would end the campaign believing they could have done more. The idea was that every player would deliver a 100 per cent every time he took the field or attended a training session or even, interestingly, a team meeting. So you didn't land up for a team meeting merely to listen and think about dinner while someone else was talking. If the 100 per cent therefore was good enough to win the World Cup that was excellent but if it wasn't good enough then so be it. The team would be proud of having done the best it could. It comes back to the truth that there is no shame in losing if you have done the best you can.

Such goals can inspire teams and it is something that leaders must think about.

Setting Up a Goal Is As Important As Scoring a Goal

The thought inherent to Waugh's approach is that each player does the best he can for the overall good of the team. There is therefore an individual goal but it is subservient to the larger goal of the team. That is what all teams seek to achieve and very few actually do. In the heat of the battle can you pass or will you go for goal, and therefore the attendant glory, yourself? It is not an easy question to answer since sport and corporate life glorify individual performance within the overall team endeavour. We want to score centuries, the goal in the big cup final, the award at the annual sales review. Indeed we must have individual goals, for that is what drives us. However, the key is in ensuring that such individual goals do not come in the way of the overall team goal. This topic has been dealt with in detail later in the book.

Team goals are often the result of several small activities performed diligently and successfully. Very few games are won by the lone warrior performing heroic deeds. That is for scripted movies and may it always be that way. Often critical roles are played by people you never see at the end. It could be a diligent finance executive who saw the need to restructure loans, a batsman who didn't score too many runs but blunted the opposition fast bowler, a left-back who spent ninety minutes marking the opposition winger. These players could remain in the shadows, away from the stars in the arclights, but they know, as do the stars, that without them playing the quiet unfashionable roles, victory would have been impossible. Often a player may be required to fail in order that another succeeds. A pacemaker in a long distance race for example sets the pace early on to ensure that the star sets a good time but in doing so he has to bow out of the race before it ends. It is not a glorious sight but it is a role that must be played by one so that the other wins. One brand may have to bear the brunt of the competition so that another brand succeeds. That brand manager might have done a fantastic job even though his brand lost. The workhorse might have to bowl into the breeze so that the strike bowler can take wickets with the wind behind him.

These are seemingly unpopular or relatively less acknowledged roles and yet they must be played. In such a situation it is imperative that the leader makes it clear to everyone what his or her role is and what the successful completion of the role entails. If that role is clearly defined and is known to everyone on the team, and therefore there is glory in carrying it out, it becomes easier to play. If the mid-fielders don't keep floating the ball into the six-yard box the strikers or forwards would find it very difficult to score.

This was rather dramatically illustrated by the arrival, at Arsenal Football Club, of a German mid-fielder of Turkish origin. Arsenal had decent forwards but they didn't seem to be getting the ball coming their way often enough. Then Mesut Ozil arrived from Real Madrid and all of a sudden, even though he hardly scored one himself, the forwards were scoring many goals. Hitherto, they had no one to set up a goal and so, couldn't score one. Maybe a very good supply chain manager can do that, or even someone who handles logistics and ensures everything else is in place.

However, in a situation where credit tends to go only to the finisher, the person who sets it up for him could well be tempted to ask for a reversal of roles—where one day he finishes and the regular finisher sets it up for him. In a manufacturing company, on-time production might well be the key to sales but if they interchange roles there would be chaos. Hence the importance lies not just in assigning roles but in the acknowledgement of their success. For every goal that is scored there is a goal that has been set up. If each of the eleven players wants to score the goal himself, nobody will.

Production always sets it up for distribution; distribution ensures that sales completes the cycle and brings home the revenue. The air force sets it up for the army to conquer territory. Bowlers bring down the target score that allows the batsmen to win the game. A great script-writer produces the lines that draw applause for the actor. Somebody has to set up a goal for someone to score it and organisations that do not reward those that set up goals will find there are no more goals to score! Clear definition of roles and communicating these to all involved is the key to a great team performance.

The huge scale at which businesses operate these days is throwing up unique challenges for managers. Firstly, teams are spread over different continents and time-zones and a number of multinational consultancies have what are called back offices in India. Typically, the managers in back offices support the client facing managers based in the US or Europe with research and analysis. Indians are best at number-crunching after all! The problem arises when these poor backroom boys spend long nights preparing one-page summaries as ready reckoners but get neither feedback nor a chance to know the outcome of their effort. The US office has the big goal spelt out but the youngsters down the line are totally disconnected from it. When you have hundreds of such talented but disillusioned young people, it must certainly be an HR manager's nightmare! Knowing your role and how it contributes to the overall goal is absolutely critical to motivation.

Goals

- Goals are dreams with deadlines.
- Goals can be out of reach but not out of sight.
- The goals you set tell the world what kind of person you are.
- What you achieve is a function of what you think you can.
- As players become bigger, their goals become more precise.
- Performance goals make you focus on the variables that can be controlled.
- Individual goals must always be aligned with team goals.
- Setting up a goal is as important as scoring a Goal.
- Clarity of the role and the goal is critical to winning.

The Winning Triangle—Ability, Attitude and Passion

If you only ever give 90 per cent in training then you will only ever give 90 per cent when it matters.

—Michael Owen

'Business,' Jack Welch says, 'is a game and winning it is a total blast.' It is. There can be few things more uplifting than when mind and body come together in victory, in a melange of emotions that has no parallel. It could be the Olympics where you have waited four years for a moment that could have cruelly passed you by, it could be winning the World Cup, or the Oscar night where uncertainty gives way to the dramatic realisation that you have made it. It could be winning an account you have aspired to for years or it could even be the result of your first competitive examination. Winning seems to make everything worth it. Certainly so when you have played the game fairly.

Yet, winning is like a welcome drink going down your throat, or like a beautiful embrace. It is brilliant while it lasts but that isn't forever. The high eventually melts away and the journey of life begins afresh. The truly remarkable among us visit these highs periodically; winning then becomes a journey, a graph where each point is crucial but is in reality merely part of a larger curve.

Winning is not a destination in itself but a series of destinations where fresh challenges are encountered and overcome along the way. Not everybody can do it, for winning can also be exhausting and that is why the true champions stand apart. These are people who not only conquer the opposition, but who also conquer themselves, since winning brings with it its own set of challenges. That is why you remember Sampras, Federer and Djokovic, Tendulkar and Warne, Nicklaus and Woods, Pele and Maradona, Vishwanathan Anand and Mary Kom. That is why you remember Infosys and Hero Honda, the Tatas, Hindustan Unilever, Reliance, GE, Apple and Google and the many large corporations around the world who make winning a habit; not an event but a series of events.

Winning is fascinating to study because of the many shades it paints life in; the challenges of winning once and the many more complex challenges of winning again. That is why champions are extraordinary people. That is why corporations that win over decades are looked up to by their peers. While winning requires you to understand your environment, it requires you, more than anything else, to understand yourself.

'Self-awareness is very important,' says the serious-minded Ajinkya Rahane. 'What works for you doesn't work for someone else.'[1] Rahane is in the habit of maintaining a diary where he makes jottings on every day of play or practice. It gives him a good idea of what contributes to a good performance and what he needs to do to get into the right frame of mind. Notes in a written-down form ensure that he doesn't forget anything, given his busy schedule and make a quick, last-minute read possible.

Talent Alone Is Not Enough

The popular perception is that great players are blessed with incredible talent. They often are, but that is not necessarily the only quality they possess. The world of sport is full of stories of brilliant talent that dazzled the world and faded away, shooting stars who attracted attention as much for their incandescence as for the brevity of their existence. The great players marry their extraordinary talent to something far more powerful, something more critical to their success. They are possessed of a wonderful attitude, a work ethic that causes them to chisel away at their craft, removing one rough edge after another till the polished diamond emerges. The romantic stories about sportsmen just landing up and demolishing the opposition, of mathematicians conjuring up beautiful proofs, of writers banging at their keyboards on a whim and producing a masterpiece are as mythical as Atlantis, the lost continent. They do more harm to young minds than anything else. As Dr. Shailesh Ayyangar says, 'A talented individual without the right attitude can't be a long-term sustainable winner. A person with great attitude but with limited talent could still be a great champion member of the team. A combination of these two will make the person a real winner.'

Sachin Tendulkar once went to a Test match venue four days in advance to practice against a particular kind of ball that he expected to face in the game. India were due to play Australia in Chennai and in the warm-up game in Mumbai he noticed that Shane Warne didn't go round the wicket to him even once. He thought to himself that Warne was probably saving that for the Test match, and so hour upon hour he worked away at playing leg spinners bowling that angle, realising the need to be perfect. When the first leg break that he faced from round the wicket in the match was despatched over mid-wicket the world went 'wow' and raised a toast to his incredible talent. It wasn't just talent, it was good old-fashioned perseverance. Admittedly, someone else with the same degree of preparation may not have been able to produce as stunning a result, but it is just as true that without the effort, his ability might have been wasted. In fact, Tendulkar's success recipe is a large tablespoon of talent but several large tablespoonfuls of attitude and of work ethic. It is heartening to see youngsters like Rahane and Virat Kohli take the game forward with a similar work ethic. A young player in the Royal Challengers

Bangalore team gaped at Kohli's training methods and his adherence to his practice and diet. Kohli is another example of great talent achieving results by being married to a great work ethic.

You must have come across those who are capable of hard work and discipline but only when they have a specific goal before them. It is like students who normally fool around but study very hard when the board exams draw near. But opportunity doesn't always knock before presenting itself and if you are not ready, you will not be able to cash in. V. V. S. Laxman told us about a Hyderabad player who wasn't getting picked for the state team and in his frustration allowed his work ethic to suffer. When an unexpected opportunity came, he found that he wasn't match-ready and hardly got an opportunity again.

Talent opens no more than the first door, occasionally the second. Players armed with talent and nothing else struggle at the third door. By the time the fourth door appears they are no longer in the picture. The most striking and sad story in Indian cricket is that of Vinod Kambli who was abundantly blessed, had put in sincere hard work through very difficult times but struggled to adjust his game to the demands of international cricket after his extraordinary entry. He had the talent, but perhaps could not show the determination and discipline required to play at the highest level.

Abhinav Bindra, India's gold medallist in shooting believes hard work and determination are the key to success whereas talented people rely too much on their ability alone. Talent takes you up to a certain level, but at the end of the day it's hard work that gets you through. You have to push yourself day in and day out. 'I was the most unathletic, uncoordinated and laid back person and not naturally gifted but I had the ability to work hard and push myself, day after day and that I believe was my talent,' adds Bindra.[2]

People who are able to marry their work ethic to their talent rise above everybody else. It is the story of almost every successful person. Tiger Woods worked harder than anyone else on perfecting his swing, while Michael Jordan's training sessions are the stuff of legend.

In 2014, following a string of poor performances, there were doubts over Saina Nehwal's career.

Saina admits she herself contemplated quitting the game. A courageous move that involved changing cities—Hyderabad to Bengaluru and a much-talked about change in coaches—Gopichand to Vimal Kumar ensured that Saina got the personal attention she thought she needed. It all worked out for Saina when she became World No. 1, won the China and India Open and reached the finals of All England and World Championships. What is not documented is that Saina sacrificed the comfort of a luxurious home and cars in Hyderabad and opted to live in a small room within the stadium premises in Bengaluru to focus on her game. It's one thing to want to win, quite another to do whatever it takes to get there.

To return to talent and the doors it can no longer

open; when you are a fourteen-year-old, your natural ability separates you from the others in your age group and allows you to be selected to the next level. Maybe you will walk through the under-seventeens as well. By the time you reach the under-nineteens, almost everybody is good, and all have emerged through a similar examination. Talent is a good friend to possess but not the discriminating factor. As Malcolm Gladwell so delightfully points out in his wonderful work *Outliers*, beyond a point it does not matter how good you are in absolute terms but merely whether you are good enough because by now other qualities become necessary. For a young batsman it probably now means analysing the bowler and being patient enough to tide over a good spell, whereas earlier his *modus operandi* would have been to demolish the bowler. It now probably is better to learn to leave balls alone till the bowler delivers where the batsman wants him to. Maybe he even acknowledges the skill of his opponent and plays chess with him rather than treating him as an opponent in the boxing ring to be knocked out as quickly as possible. There is this delicious story told about a sixteen-year-old Tendulkar who went to Pakistan with the Indian team and had to be told that at this level bowlers needed to be respected; it wasn't something he had ever worried about, because no bowler had really challenged him until then.

Young managers discover that their ability to find patterns in data, to produce outstanding funds flow statements, to devise complex algorithms, are soon matched for importance by whether or not they can get along with people, by whether they can communicate to the rest of the world, by whether they can lead teams and display qualities of empathy, maybe ruthlessness. Lawyers find that their courtroom demeanour could count for as much as their legal knowledge, a surgeon's bedside manners could reassure a nervous patient. Ability brings people up to a certain position in the management hierarchy but now they discover that they need to possess completely different or at least distantly related skills to go further up.

'Spin is no more a mystery,' says R. Ashwin. 'You tend to watch a lot of videos and the batsman knows exactly what cues to take. It's not about skill anymore. There are bowlers all over the world who are good at their art, know how to pick up wickets. What separates you from the rest is how well you handle pressure and how brave you can be in testing times.'[3]

Which brings us to the interesting question of what is a skill? Is it merely about batting and bowling or writing code or analyzing markets? Or would, as Ashwin points out, handling pressure also qualify as a skill? Organisations hire based on 'functional skills' but in trying situations soft skills become critical differentiators. Handling pressure, resilience, optimism or even being a team player can be counted as essential skills and organizations need to find ways to check for these when they recruit or even promote employees.

During one of our sessions for a top auto components

company, a gentleman got up to ask a perfectly valid question. 'When the company was starting out, they recruited us. We did well. Then, when it became bigger, they said we will recruit only from the IIMs. Now they are saying we want to become a global company so we want people with foreign MBAs. What I want to ask is: if we were not good, the company would not have become big in the first place, so why should we not get the new bigger assignments?' In a simplistic world what he stated would be absolutely right. However, as you move up the leadership ladder you need a different perspective and wider skills. Perhaps the gentleman was excellent when the company was of a certain size, but wasn't too effective in a changed environment. Hopefully, he would have realised that it wasn't about an 'IIM degree' but about acquiring newer skills.

The world has changed so much in the last few years that middle and senior managers are struggling to stay relevant. Much of what they studied isn't valid anymore so there's is a lot to learn as well as unlearn. While it's easier to get familiar with social media and digital technology or get a grip on cloud and big data, ego comes in the way of the unlearning bit. Those who went to B-School are all too familiar with the concept of 'batch parity' and that is a tough one to unlearn! Today it's possible you might have to report to someone younger and on paper, less qualified than you. Those who have seen a fair bit of success find it particularly difficult to accept that what brought them success is not going to work anymore. Sandip Das believes it's possible to stay relevant if you are curious and not worried about the age of the person teaching you! In fact as an investor and mentor, he spends time every day with aspiring entrepreneurs, learning in the process about new technology, an experience he calls 'blood transfusion'. No wonder then, A. S. Ramchander lists 'the skill to work with people who know more than yourself' as one that will be critical for leaders of the future.[4]

Resources Versus Resourcefulness

Therefore, it is not the talent alone or the resources that players possess that is critical, as much as knowing what to do with them. This determines whether or not they become champions. There was a time in India when possession of resources was a differentiating factor. Few had access to credit. Quality education wasn't available outside the big cities. It wasn't how good you were but what you had or where you were that determined your future. As a result, young men instead of setting up industries on their own, worked for those that already had industries; cricketers who lived in small towns didn't have access to the best coaching methods and were in awe of the city boys who, armed with the opportunity that their birth and their address had given them, filled up almost all the places in the Indian team. As late as 1983, India's World Cup winning team had players from five cities only; when we graduated from IIM-A in 1985, nobody ever spoke of starting out on their own. By the time India had won the World T20 in 2007, players from nine towns were represented and fresh management graduates routinely dabbled in entrepreneurship. More and more students joining the IITs hail from smaller towns. M. S. Dhoni once famously said that players from small towns are tougher because they try harder.

With high quality television and good commentators taking cricket into the remotest parts of India, young players were exposed to the latest trends and the latest ideas. Armed with this and the prosperity seeping into the next rung of towns—no longer fettered by self-doubt—young men, from smaller towns, more ambitious, more driven to doing what it takes, began flooding Indian cricket. Indeed, they now had access to a resource that the city boys no longer had—time. They had the space to play, they didn't have to make do with a little corridor between two large buildings. So, whether it was getting into the Indian team, or into institutes of higher learning the tide had begun to turn.

We have now reached a stage in the country where resources are far more freely available. Delightful statements that we thought we would never hear have done the rounds—that it was the idea, not the funds behind the idea that was critical because funds could be organised, but the idea, not always. This has changed the way we do business, but more critically it has changed the kind of people who do business. With resources being more easily accessible, and no longer being the differentiator they once were, it is how you use the resources that matters more. It is not who you are but what you can do that is important; resourcefulness is now the discriminant, to borrow a term from statistics.

Till the pre-start-up era, resources were the wings that allowed you to dream. There was a high degree of correlation between your aspiration and the funds you possessed. Managers based their targets on the budgets that were allocated; you had to have more to deliver more. The entrepreneurship wave came and changed the thinking. Bright youngsters with great ideas but empty pockets had dreams of changing the world. Their aspirations were way beyond what their resources justified. In Prof. C. K. Prahlad's eyes, this was what differentiated the entrepreneurial mindset from the managerial one.

While resources are necessary—and even start-ups require VC support beyond a point, an abundance of resources can make teams lax. It's not so much about how much you have but just the comfort and security of knowing that you could get away with being a bit careless. Bootstrapping was not a term that you would hear in an MBA course till recently. The disruptive nature of technology and resultant effect on cost structures is forcing established businesses to be big but act small. The 'frugality mindset' advocated by the low-cost yet most profitable carrier, Indigo Airlines is not commonly seen in large organizations.

In cricket too, countries like India and Australia have

more funds and a large pool of players to choose from, but New Zealand is a country with a small population where cricket is not even the number one sport. Their former captain, Stephen Fleming says that from a very early age they are taught to make the most of the limited resources they have. This is apparent when you see how much more they win than they are expected to, making them a well-respected team all over the world. Former England captain Nasser Hussain regards them very highly, 'since they always punch above their weight'. When Stephen Fleming came to India to be with Chennai Super Kings he said he was awestruck by the abundance of talented players around him, a situation he had never faced in New Zealand.

This flattening of the world, this levelling of the playing field, fuelled by the internet and the 'google-isation' of the world forces us to ask ourselves what kind of people or organisations we are. Are we high on ability but questionable on attitude? Or are we only moderately gifted (in relative terms, of course) but make the most of what we have? Are we therefore, slack organisations or stretch organisations? Do we rely on resources or on our resourcefulness? India's cricketers, or for that matter Indian industry, turned the corner when they started becoming resourceful; when they became agile, worldly-wise and confident.

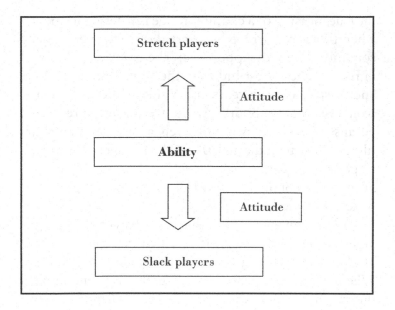

Winning in All Conditions

Maybe it is symbolic of their attitude, their adaptability, or their resourcefulness, but good teams are capable of winning in all conditions. In cricket, you will find a number of teams who historically have been much better playing in home conditions, but seem listless when travelling or playing in more challenging surroundings. India, for example won a mere 5 Tests out of 80 played overseas in the decade spanning the eighties and nineties while New Zealand won only 8 away Tests from 2000 till the end of the decade, 7 of which were against Zimbabwe and Bangladesh. These were decent teams but the true measure of a champion side is whether it can win when things are arrayed against them: weather, playing conditions, crowd support etc. The two defining teams in recent times, West Indies in the seventies and eighties and Australia in the years either side of the millennium, won everywhere. South Africa were hugely respected because they remained unbeaten away for nine years till they lost to India in 2015. Their players were well-respected too with four of their batsmen averaging over 50 in away conditions and Dale Steyn bowling like the wind everywhere.

Good companies are like that too, always creating value and putting in the most effort when market conditions are hostile. In a long bull run, everyone makes money. When insurance opened up, virtually everyone jumped on the bandwagon and made profits. When words like sub-prime were unknown you only had to insert the word 'software' in the name of your company to get the meter ticking. However, spring inevitably gives way to winter, resources start to thin and then your ability to be resourceful comes to the fore. We are already seeing that happening. Large organizations are struggling to maintain margins and market shares while start-ups that were having a good ride are realizing that funds are no longer that easy to come by. Adaptability in changing circumstances then would be essential to survival.

Australia showed the stuff they were made of during their outstanding World Cup campaign in 2003. They were faced with a couple of tricky matches at the start, against India and Pakistan, and were likely to miss two star players, Michael Bevan, who hadn't yet recovered from injury, and Darren Lehmann who was suspended. On the morning of their first game came the news that the great Shane Warne had failed a drug test conducted earlier in Australia and was due to fly back home. Most teams would have carried that state of mind onto the ground; they might have pondered over what could have been instead of what really was. Instead, Australia rallied together and produced one of their best performances ever.

The confidence of having won under the most demanding circumstances carried them on the crest of a wave that brought them the World Cup. When the going got tough, the champions had shown their worth. They had the bench strength but they were able to respond to a difficult situation very quickly.

The highly respected Cadbury company found itself in a similar situation in 2003. Just before the festive season of Diwali, when sales normally go up by 15 per cent, they were hit by the 'worms' controversy. Some consumers complained that their favourite Dairy Milk bars were infested with worms. For a family brand like Cadbury, it could have been a disaster and for a while it was. They addressed the problem directly, explained where the infestation might have come from, invested substantially in new tamper-proof packaging, began an exercise to rekindle trust with the consumer and in doing so actually emerged stronger from a potentially catastrophic situation. 'While we're talking about a few bars of the 30 million we sell every month—we believe that to be a responsible company, consumers need to have complete faith in products. So even if it calls for substantial investment and change, one must not let the consumers' confidence erode,' the then managing director Bharat Puri said.[5] Cadbury had the resources but it was their agility, their ability to size up a situation and take immediate action that saved the day.

Australia's cricketers and Cadbury's managers showed that champions can, and must, scrap as well. It is not a quality that the hugely talented always possess; sometimes talent gets bored when confronted by a situation it doesn't really fancy. You will see that with complaining divas. Champions dig deep; when the first serve isn't really working, when the leg break isn't coming out of the hand the right way, when the wind picks up just at tee off and drags the first shot wide, champions show the virtues of hanging in there. When the booming cover drive or the elegant flick through mid-wicket isn't really on, champions will scrape, nudging here and there for a run or just blocking for long periods. They are willing to play like royalty, even for a morsel of food. Everybody looks good when they are on top of their game but as Martina Navratilova once remarked, 'What matters,' she said, 'isn't how well you play when you're playing well. What matters is how well you play when you're playing badly.' This is something we must all ask ourselves because when conditions are arrayed against us, we sometimes give up. We know of teams that left on assignments believing they had no chance and it came as no surprise that they lost.

How good is the food when a chef is cooking badly? An article, when the columnist is going through writer's block? While an average player looks brilliant when playing well but thoroughly abysmal when bad, a champion's head is always above water.

Australia and Cadbury, like so many others, are examples of teams that achieved success consistently and success is the most powerful addiction that the world has ever known. The heady feeling that goes with victory is unmatched across countries or cultures and you really need to experience it once to get hooked. Yet we find that the first time round, difficult as it may seem, is actually easier than the sequel. Replicating success is the biggest challenge and those who have mastered the art of doing this are the true champions.

Passion—The Final Sieve

Finally, even among people who successfully marry their ability with the winning attitude, there are a few that make it to the very top. Sachin Tendulkar, Michael Schumacher, Vishwanathan Anand, Maradona, Messi, Kohli, Usain Bolt—they managed to reign supreme in a manner that they became synonymous with the sport they played. They were in love with what they did and had a great passion to perform. Tendulkar once said in an interview that his bats spoke to him! Their domination in their field meant that they set the rules and defined the category much in the same way that brands like Xerox did and Google does. Their passion, focus and obsession with their game and performance made them stand out as the best among the best.

There is a lesson there. Some of us are as gifted in our profession as Tendulkar and Anand are in theirs. If we can similarly marry our ability with work ethic and acquire the passion they had for their craft, we too could become the Tendulkars or Anands of our profession.

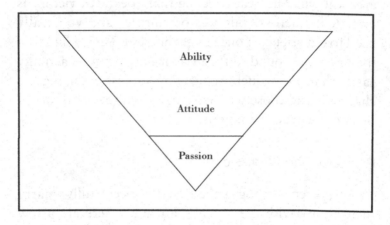

Contrary to popular perception, ability is not a major distinguishing factor in success, especially as the level of competition increases. It is fairly evenly spread out across cultures and countries. It is a fairly large base of people. The first sieve therefore is attitude and people who can marry that to ability become more successful. Skills can be more easily taught, attitude can't ... and at the very top is passion, an extraordinary drive, where success and joy come together for win after win.

The Burden of Winning

If you are succeeding all the time, you should ask yourself if you are taking enough risks. If you do not take enough risks, you may also be losing out on many opportunities.

—Azim Premji

That buzz in the dressing room, that electrifying feeling, team bonding at its highest, resources abundant and the overall positive mindset—the fruits of victory are many and varied! Victory has a momentum that is powerful enough to carry the whole team or organisation with it.

That is the key, because winning teams can wear the cloak of infallibility and have the confidence to take on any new challenge. There is an energy in the team that consumes even the bit player who has had no chance of starting. It envelopes the baggage man and the score-keeper too. Magic Johnson once famously said, 'Everybody on a championship team doesn't get publicity, but everyone can say he's a champion.' In fact in cricket-crazy India, all is forgiven when India wins a series especially against Pakistan. Predictably, it's the same in that country too! Then the coach is labelled a genius, the captain hailed as the greatest, there are celebrations all over the country, cricketers sign a fresh round of endorsements and cricket squabbles that normally make front page news are buried, at least for the moment.

Actually, there is no better time than during a winning streak to strengthen pride in the team and build loyalty. Winning teams are magnets for those in search of excellence. What better team glue than victory to keep the herd from straying and looking for greener pastures. Smart leaders use the exuberance of success to spur their team on to achieving greater glory. Sandip Das says that the camaraderie in the team extends to even helping slow performers pick up. He thinks winning teams are, '… apolitical and secure and back each other.'[1] Each of these is an interesting thought in itself. Losing teams by contrast can be racked by politics, have people looking over their shoulders and players who tend to put themselves first. If you read Rahul Dravid's piece at the end of this book, you will notice that he too agrees. He thinks winning teams are more giving and forgiving. We have heard so many clients say that when teams go through troubled times, everyone goes back into their silos and guards their turf. So does success create team spirit or does team spirit lead to success? That's something that can be debated an entire evening!

Looking Behind the Scoreboard

If you think victory seems a perfect place to rest a while, you couldn't be more wrong. It's great to win but like all sweet things in life it comes with side-effects. Many sportspeople in fact refer to it as the burden of winning. Once you have won, the world looks at you differently. The way you look at yourself changes as well. The next time you are in a contest you are the defending champion with a record and reputation to defend.

Abhinav Bindra talks of going to the London Olympics, having won the gold at the previous Olympics. 'I was reminded about my past every day. It was very challenging—remaining in the present and being detached from the gold.'[2] To relieve himself of the burden, he created what he called his motto, 'I don't need it but I want it.' Pete Sampras first won the US Open in 1990, at the age of nineteen. When he lost the title in the following year, he said at a press conference, 'It kind of takes the monkey off my back a bit.' There was almost a sense of relief. He didn't have to wake up to the responsibility of being a champion, and with the expectation that accompanies it. When you are a first-time winner like Sampras was, you sometimes have the advantage of being the surprise package. Opponents don't know too much about you and hence can be caught unawares. Winners, however, are always under scrutiny, they are expected to win, their game gets analysed threadbare and the opponent comes armed with all the information he needs. If you are a challenger you make news when you win, if you are a winner, it's news when you lose! Interestingly, when we took *The Winning Way* seminar to Infosys, this was the point that none other than Mr. Narayana Murthy picked up. He said that Infosys too had observed that they got less coverage when they did well and more when their results fell short of people's expectations.

Federer losing at Wimbledon, or indeed Djokovic in Australia are events, as are Schumacher crashing out while at his peak or Woods missing an eight foot putt when he was conquering all in front of him. It is not easy for winners to live with the knowledge that winning is merely par. Infosys or Reliance can report better results than most but will disappoint if they don't match the standards they have set for themselves. So too with the Oberoi and the Taj who must agonise over little things for fear that their absence is what will be noticed.

Sometimes though, winners can get caught up in celebrating the victory rather than analysing it. After all post-mortems are only for the dead aren't they? Jerry Rao, former Country Head, Consumer Banking, Citibank India, and founder and former CEO of Mphasis, in fact goes to the extent of saying that he is wary of people who have just come out of a successful project. He says they are 'all puffed up' and can go lax on rigour. So the next time you want to hit the bar to celebrate, wait a bit and give yourself some time to think about why and how you won. If winning was analysed as much as failure is, perhaps teams would stumble onto new insights, maybe they could establish an activity pattern that they could repeat at a later date.

It is important therefore to know why you have won because if your own victory has surprised you, it only means that you didn't expect to win, that you thought it was a chance win, or maybe because your competitor faltered or that you just got lucky. There is a lovely story of a leading striker who didn't celebrate after scoring a goal. When asked why, he said it was his job to score goals. 'Does the postman celebrate when he delivers a letter?' he is known to have asked. Success has to be repeatable because that is what makes you a champion. This implies knowing why you are winning.

Having said that, it's not merely winning that counts but also the manner in which the win was fashioned. Victories achieved under difficult and hostile circumstances carry more pride and are cherished more. Like away wins in cricket or away goals in football. Nasser Hussain was proud of winning in Pakistan as Alastair Cook was when they won in India in 2012, while Rahul Dravid was overjoyed at winning a series in England in 2007 and seemed just as happy to watch India win a test at Lords in 2014. In spite of winning against Australia in India a few times, the Test wins at Adelaide in 2003 and in Perth in 2008 were extra special, while the Australians look back at the 2004 series win in India with great pride. The Tour de France is so prestigious because it takes place under the most gruelling circumstances and is as much a test of character and team spirit as it is of cycling skills.

So while talent is always acknowledged as a quality essential to winners, words like grit, perseverance and determination are used just as often. Indeed in the foreword to Steve Waugh's autobiography *Out of My Comfort Zone*, Rahul Dravid wrote, 'Waugh gave grit a good name!' Apart from the fact that it's a great line, it also provides valuable insight. Flair has always been considered glamorous, but grit has never been fashionable, and certainly not in India.

Real champions like to play in adverse conditions from time to time just to prove themselves. Grand Slam winners have so much respect because they have succeeded in all conditions and have been able to adapt their game to the differing demands of grass and clay. Marathon runners participate in runs all over the world and in different climatic conditions, altitudes and terrain. Dravid rates a century in England very high because it was scored when the conditions were stacked against him. And Tendulkar's extraordinary longevity meant that he was good enough when fit and hurt, in good form and during a struggle, on seaming pitches, turners and featherbeds. This ability separates the champions from the challengers. In fact when the going is good everyone does well, but when the going is tough that's when you separate the men from the boys, as with the cricketers who do wonderfully well on the subcontinent but fail on bouncy wickets, with the reverse being just as true. This is as true in the stock market as it is in sport. Warren Buffet said, 'Only when the tide goes out do you discover who's been swimming naked.'[3] Of the hundreds of companies that sprung up during the internet boom, the solid IT companies survived and flourished despite the stock market crash (around the turn of the century), while several 'get rich quick' dotcoms bit the dust, their fancy ESOPs reduced to mere scraps of paper.

To return to the burden of winning. Once you have been labelled a winner you are expected to perform like a champion every single time. Often, not all successful people can handle the pressure that comes with these raised expectations. Since it is impossible to perform at peak when under great pressure, it's possible for people to crumble and fall apart. Boris Becker, who won Wimbledon at 17 was candid enough to say that if he had won his first Slam title at 21, he might actually have won more than he eventually did. Maybe he thought he would have been readier to handle the side-effects of winning.

We often talk about the 'third year' in international sport being critical. When a newcomer comes along you don't always know what he can do, or what bag of tricks he possesses. By the second year you have sorted him out and he now faces a situation, new to him, where he has to confront failure and find a way around it, ideally by developing new skills or by becoming more consistent. The better players succeed in year three while the flash-in-the-pan kind wither away, unable to come to terms with the heightened challenge.

The Side-Effects of Winning

The media is known to be partial to winners. The performance of a winner is dissected and discussed in full public view. Champions need to be strong and grounded with so much attention and adulation aimed at them, so as not to allow it to go to their heads. You run the risk of believing everything you read and hear about yourself; as Jerry Rao said, you run the risk of getting puffed up. You see that with footballers in England and most definitely with young cricketers in India who are sometimes so much in love with what they want to hear that they only befriend those who tell them those things. Post the IPL, which sometimes allows for instant riches and fame, staying grounded became a challenge for young players.

Often, when the goal is daunting and the journey arduous, there is a sense of having achieved the goal, even if it's really only a milestone. You see that with students who work so hard to make it to the IITs and IIMs and experience burnout once they get there. Sadly, they mistake a milestone for a goal and they feel that their destination has already arrived. It is true of young Indian cricketers who sometimes experience such joy and relief at being selected that they are not ready for what follows. Even companies are known to become complacent once they become market leaders. It's easier for the number two and three to remain motivated since there is still an unfulfilled feeling and a higher sense of purpose. That is why managing success is always more difficult than achieving it and staying number one is more difficult than becoming number one.

On a macro-level, Australia began benchmarking themselves beyond their era in order to create challenges. They asked themselves whether they could be spoken of in the same breath as Don Bradman's 1948 Invincibles. The Invincibles were the first Australian Test side to have toured England and come back unbeaten. They won every single one of the thirty-two games that were played. Incidentally, it was also Don Bradman's last tour of England.

On a more micro-level, Brett Lee says they trained as if they were number two to inject the urgency needed into a daily, routine affair. 'There were days when we knew we could train a bit and win. On those days we probably trained for two-and-a-half hours or sometimes only for one hour but we went particularly flat out, pretending as if we were number two.' A number of innovations like throwing with the wrong arm were introduced thereby making the otherwise uninteresting training sessions more challenging.

Keeping large corporate teams hungry is a bigger issue as leaders find it difficult to spend sufficient time with their teams. Dr. Santrupt Mishra of the Aditya Birla Group who is from a rare species of HR leaders who became business leaders says, 'Leadership's role is empowering and encouraging people and tolerance of failure. Whenever you encourage people to keep that hunger alive, that hunger will manifest itself in many ways and in the pursuit of that hunger some would fail. How you react to that failure decides if you can keep that hunger alive or you kill the hunger.'[4]

N. V. Thyagarajan, COO, Genpact, warns of another danger, 'potential arrogance'. Failure brings with it a certain humility and a desire to improve. We don't know if Bill Gates spoke from experience but he certainly spoke well when he said, 'Success is a lousy teacher, it seduces smart people into thinking they can't lose.' When Coca Cola re-entered India in 1993 they probably expected consumers to welcome them back with open arms. Instead, they faced competition from unlikely quarters. Pepsi might be Coke's only major rival the world over, but in India, Thums Up, a homegrown brand from Parle, was tough to dislodge. A few years later Coke bought out Thums Up hoping to fight Pepsi but when that strategy too didn't work, they unsuccessfully tried to kill the brand. Thums Up, India's largest-selling cola brand, still belongs to Coke and was eventually given the full advertising and marketing support that it deserves.

Success becomes a blanket that covers up weaknesses. You don't see them growing until one fine day, the blanket is ripped off to reveal reality. In Hyderabad, there is a popular saying, *oopar sherwani, andar pareshani*. In other words, the finery outside conceals the penury within.

Never Change a Winning Combination?

The success blanket is probably at the heart of the expression 'never change a winning combination.' It's tempting and so easy, so typical of human behaviour, that we've all probably done it at some point in our careers. Having won, no one really wants to rock the boat. Innovation at this stage seems risky (it always is but seems riskier when you believe you've cracked the magic formula) and experimentation seems unnecessary. Why fix something when it ain't broken? Unfortunately, things have sometimes started to break and nobody has noticed this happening.

In any winning team for example, there are a few under-performers, along with many over-achievers. In fact, all teams have their share of under- and over-performers. It's the ratio that varies across teams and decides how good they can be. Just because the team has won, it would be foolish to continue carrying deadwood. It's easier to cull when the team is down since it's not debated and anyway people expect that to happen. It is just as imperative when the team is winning and the mood is celebratory. Australia did that well. They let a great sportsperson like Ian Healy go as soon as it became apparent that his time was up. As indeed they did with other legends like Steve Waugh in 2004 and Adam Gilchrist in 2012.

The underlying assumption in the concept of a winning combination is that there is a formula that worked well for you once and that it will continue to work again irrespective of how much time has elapsed between then and now and the circumstances that it worked under. The fact is, success is always in the context of time, space and scale, of when, where and at what level. You need to look at the context in which success was achieved. If that has changed, then the probability of the same formula working has perhaps changed too. It might still work, but it is not necessary that it will.

Success is in the Context of Time, Space and Scale

Pyaasa was a haunting film but unlikely to appeal to a generation that doesn't think too much of black-and-white photography, poetry and romantic losers. Bjorn Borg could never win Wimbledon with his old wooden Donnay racket in today's era where over-sized rackets generate such tremendous speed and power. Batsmen who were told to 'give the first hour to the bowlers' in a Test match would discover there are only twenty minutes left thereafter in a T20 game. Alternately, sloggers who routinely clobber the ball over cow corner may not have managed too many against the four-pronged West Indies pace bowling attack.

Eventually, it is about giving the consumers what they want and those requirements may have changed. T20 cricket is an excellent example of contemporary packaging for a traditional product to appeal to newer consumers. So too was the relaunch of Lifebuoy without its traditional odour. In both cases, managers could have stuck with what had worked in the past but they realised that the reason they were successful may no longer be relevant. The passage of time is a huge factor to keep in mind while determining the relevance of a success formula. It came as no surprise when Sundar Pichai, CEO of Google, on a visit to India in 2016, kept harping on the theme of relevance in a rapidly changing world.

The brochures that mutual fund managers send out have a disclaimer that says: past performance is no guarantee for future success. What worked at one time, as we have seen, may not work at a later date. What worked in one market need not work in another either. If McDonalds had to succeed in India, it could not do so with its beef or pork burgers, it had to invent the McAloo Tikki burger to cater to vegetarians. Similarly, Marico had to modify its hair oil formulations and create creams and gels for the Middle-East markets where the smell of coconut oil was not acceptable.

In days gone by, England routinely played county seamers on India's dusty tracks and India brought four spinners with them in the first half of an English season in 1996, when it could get really cold and spinners struggled even to grip the ball. A batsman who plunders bowling on slow, low Indian wickets may not always do well on bouncy or fast tracks. So success must be viewed in the context of *where* as much as *when*. For example, Wimbledon and the French Open are played on different surfaces and with the exception of a few Grand Slam winners, only some have adapted to both equally well.

Those who rigidly hold on to a winning formula are likely to discover that success does not last forever. Companies with traditional distribution strengths discovered with the arrival of e-commerce and digitisation that they had to adapt because with people buying directly, the trade, as they knew it, ran the risk of becoming irrelevant. Batsmen with a strike rate of 50, perfectly acceptable in test cricket, found they needed to take it up to about 90 or even 100 in one-day cricket and even as high as 140 in T20. Only the very best are able to display sufficient expertise in each format.

If there is a process that you used when production was at level x, it's unlikely that it would be just as effective at 2x, 3x and so on. This is one of the challenges before small enterprises seeking to upscale. Apart from production processes, which are an obvious issue, there is also the question of manpower. Deep Kalra, the pioneering founder of the popular travel portal MakeMyTrip.com learnt that as teams get larger, maintaining similar value systems becomes increasingly difficult. 'It started getting difficult after we grew beyond 150-200 staff members. While you hope that by hiring the right kind of senior managers and managers with the right passion and values, and imbuing them with your sense of passion, the osmosis would work down the line. But it doesn't work that way and the training and development losses are quite high. Also every manager has his/her own style of working so things tend to get distorted as you grow bigger and are perforce not able to spend as much time with rank and file.'[5] You can already hear murmurs of the same kind of disillusionment being experienced by youngsters in start-ups that were considered hot and happening less than five years ago.

Young cricketers discover too that what worked at one level may not at another. In international cricket, bad balls are hard to come by, and so acquiring patience and the ability to pick the right ball to hit becomes critical. The style that worked at first-class level may no longer produce a long innings for them. So too with young bowlers who can sometimes expect to get away with a bad ball. At Test level the first one they bowl might be hammered away. Discipline with line and length becomes critical as they move up a level. Success also needs to be measured at the level, or scale, at which it was achieved.

Not everything needs to be thrown out of the window though. It's a good idea to revisit what worked for you, evaluate what still works and then, discard the rest. That is why we believe that it is important to analyse success with the same rigour with which failure is assessed. If you don't know why you've won you will not know what changes to make. As Sandy Gordon, Australian sports psychologist who has had many successful sessions with cricketers and teams says, 'Like all athletes, and coaches as well, we only tend to analyse failure. What I did (with the Australian team) was oblige people to analyse success a bit more—why did you play well today? Why did you get a hundred? Why did you get a five-for? ... and getting people to reflect. Very often there is a pattern of behaviour, a pattern of thinking, a pattern of emotions which many are unaware of.' It is something that all of us would do well to contemplate!

The Perils of Winning

Some winners display a streak of arrogance and can start to believe that since they were good in one sphere or area of business, they would automatically succeed in another as well. Several successful sportspersons who tried their hand at films or politics found these professions to be a completely different ball game and not one that they could master very easily. Michael Jordan probably thought on the same lines when he temporarily gave up basketball for his ill-fated dalliance with baseball. As he discovered, the skills required in a new area of activity may be quite different from the ones you possess and could be of little consequence in the new venture. Organisations find that out when they diversify irrationally. Business houses make a foray into media ventures, for example, and meet with limited or no success. Companies with strengths in infrastructure may not succeed in the service sector. Those that have done well in B2B businesses needn't do as well in consumer-driven businesses. A strong presence in corporate and investment banking in India did not translate into a sustained retail business for Bank of America, and NDTV's successful news channel could not ensure a similar triumph for its forays in the lifestyle channel segment. Sportsmen, used to having things done for them, can find life a struggle after they have retired and need, in a manner of speaking, to sell themselves. They could still succeed but it is not a great assumption to make.

Success also comes with trappings, happy ones initially but ones that can make you lose your focus on winning. Net practice gives way to ribbon-cutting, photo-ops etc. Society has a way of heaping undeserved accolades on winners, making them more attractive than they really are. Winning a championship suddenly makes a player 'suave,' 'sexy,' 'stylish' and more such in the same vein. The perks and trappings of success make the champion forget what it was that made him a champion in the first place. It's difficult for people who experience a sudden upgrade in lifestyle and social status not to get carried away by it all and they sometimes lose it completely. Geet Sethi in his thought-provoking book *Success Vs. Joy* speaks of this. He says, 'Most sportsmen initially play for the sheer joy of playing. Somewhere along the line, some of them start playing to the gallery. That's when things go downhill. Once you start playing for what you think society wants from you, you get sucked into the sins of pride and arrogance.' Ego and arrogance are particularly dangerous in an increasingly volatile and uncertain world where nobody is too big to fail and tough questions need to be asked and answered. A stable team enveloped by the warm and happy glow of success may not always be alert enough to notice that their radars have got switched off. Increasingly companies are discovering that missing one trend can set them back many years, maybe even turn out to be fatal as Kodak found when they missed the digital trend and Nokia did when they missed out on smartphones and dual-sim phones.

In winning teams sometimes, conversations can get limited to what they are doing; the talk is all about how good they are (which is good sometimes) and no one wants to rock the boat. Instead of saying what they believe in, people can start talking about what they think people want to hear. This inward thinking can box teams in and leave them vulnerable when erstwhile challengers, sometimes looked down upon, streak past them.

In fact, we often talk about the three related perils of winning: ego, over-confidence and complacency. Teams that win consistently can sometimes start thinking they only need to turn up to win, can look down at the opposition and not give them the respect an opponent deserves at all times. These are teams that are ripe for the beating and that is often why you see upsets in sports; why established production houses produce duds; why otherwise prudent fund managers pick mediocre stocks. In the face of ordinary competition, teams can mistakenly start believing in their superiority and can end up offering only 50 per cent. When this happens, a time can come when that 50 per cent is all they can offer. Michael Holding once told us about Barry Richards and that he could see why Richards had been a great cricketer but also that he could see the effect of having played against a lot of ordinary opposition. That is why the key job of a manager, or that of a captain of teams that win all the time, is to maintain the hunger, ensure they do not slip into auto-mode, that they keep these three elements of self-destruction at bay.

We often talk about how it is more dangerous to win when delivering only, say, 70 per cent. A defeat when the effort is lower can wake you up, a win with a lower threshold of effort can start making you complacent.

It is said that victory has a thousand fathers. Nothing can be truer. While there are many who want to claim credit, virtually nobody wants to accept responsibility for failure. The moment you hear of a success story, you will find relatives, friends, teachers and just about everyone giving interviews saying they were the first to spot the potential, guide the young talent, play a key role in progress and so on and so forth. In fact, successful people discover they have more relatives and friends than they thought they had. This happens with teams as well. People and departments claim that their contribution was most critical, the joy of a team win can get buried amidst the credit that various factions claim and so, in spite of the team winning, you sometimes meet disgruntled individuals who feel under-appreciated and under-rewarded. It is one of the many symptoms of what Pat Riley, legendary coach of the LA Lakers and author of *The Winner Within* refers to as the 'Disease of Me' which he says eventually leads to the 'Defeat of Us'. It is something good managers and captains must keep an eye out for.

Pat Riley's Seven Danger Signals

- Inexperience in dealing with sudden success.

- Chronic feelings of under-appreciation.

- Paranoia over being cheated out of one's rightful share.

- Resentment against the competence of partners.

- Personal effort mustered solely to outshine a team mate.

- A leadership vacuum resulting from the formation of cliques and rivalries.

- Feelings of frustration even when the team performs successfully.

Interestingly, senior managers who work closely with millenials report that three of these signals acutely manifest themselves in Gen Y. As mentioned earlier in the book, the democratisation of opportunities, while largely having had a positive impact on society has also meant that talented youngsters from less privileged backgrounds suddenly land themselves jobs with fancy salaries. Armed with rising aspirations and multiple credit cards, they are driving India's economy and in the process they are also taking on the stress of managing their EMIs. The EMI, we hear plays a central role in career decisions today.

The word that comes up pretty early in any conversation involving Gen Y is 'entitlement mindset'. Basically what it means is that this generation has been brought up feeling special, are surrounded by opportunities and won't settle for anything but the best. Something like what Aishwarya Rai said in the L'Oreal ad, 'Because I'm worth it!' No amount of appreciation seems good enough and every achievement must come with a reward attached. An HR manager in an IT company confided in us about how he was wary of praising youngsters. It is invariably followed by, 'So when am I getting a raise or a promotion?' he says. Even in a Big Four firm, we were told of how young managers felt unappreciated or frustrated even if they didn't get their pick of projects from a list of assignments, enviable by any standard, that the firm attracts.

Too Much Winning Could Be Dangerous

Some brands like Cadburys, Tata Motors and Colgate have been what we like to call, 'chronic winners' at various times. These are brands that lead with a sizeable margin and haven't been challenged too often. Companies in such situations may not really need to stretch or struggle and they probably don't remember having been seriously threatened by a competitor. They are in the position of a Sachin Tendulkar, never having to go to bed wondering if he would make it to the team the next day. Let's say they can safely take success for granted even if they perform at only 80 per cent efficiency. That's when some chronic winners get into trouble. Competitors are not exactly breathing down your neck so it might be natural to take your eyes off them just for a while maybe. Abundant resources are available at your disposal so a bit of carelessness here and there can probably go unnoticed. The going is good so the team isn't alert in noticing new trends emerging. They don't need to because times haven't exactly been tough. So if a minor challenge crops up, the team isn't geared to handle it. After a while, the fear is that the 80 per cent efficiency level that the team has got used to operating at becomes all it's capable of doing. It turns out to be a case of satisfactory under-performance in the sense that the team is still winning but the performance potential that it had is now diminished. They are ripe for a setback and they probably haven't even realized it. The year 2010 alone saw a drop in market share of over 12 per cent for both Nokia and Hero Honda making both the brands look a bit vulnerable after a long and very successful run. It needs grit and luck to claw back but sometimes the downward spiral becomes difficult to manage and the result, like with Nokia, is fatal. It is something worth contemplating. If a giant, and a respected company, like Nokia could fail because, maybe, it took its eye off the ball, then almost everyone is vulnerable.

'Satisfactory underperformance', to borrow a term from management guru Sumantra Ghoshal, is a far more dangerous illness than might seem apparent. Apart from getting people to function or work well below their ability it can spread like a virus through an organisation.

In a sports team for example, it could be the attitude to training and preparation before a game. Just as young players emulate outstanding work ethic, so too can they start believing that it is permissible for talent to be sloppy. If senior players have late nights, you can be sure the youngsters will be tagging along soon. If the senior manager is loath to prove himself before his juniors it can lead to a cascading effect, which is why the old captaincy story from cricket continues to hold true—never ask your players to do something you wouldn't do yourself. Satisfactory underperformance is a serious illness with winning teams and like some infections can stay below the surface until it is too late.

That is why Nitin Paranjpe thinks organisations need to have a healthy paranoia. He believes winning teams need to benchmark ruthlessly every time and the reason they sometimes don't is that they remain too internally focused. They spend too much time and energy worrying about what is happening inside the company rather than what is happening outside it. His healthy paranoia, for example, is about widening gaps because 'if you don't, you don't acquire the tailwinds that will take you further. If, for example I reach a million outlets and competition reaches 500,000, if I then grow to 1.1 million I can be happy that I have grown 10 per cent but in the same time if the opposition starts reaching 800,000 my lead is effectively cut, my gap hasn't widened.' Healthy paranoia would seem to be a good antidote to satisfactory underperformance. Sundar Pichai was probably thinking on similar lines when he suggested that we must surround ourselves with people better than us. 'Never be secure. People better than you will push you to do better,' he said.[6]

Winning teams can also get into comfort zones and sometimes stagnate in terms of growth rate. Along with creating the vision for the next level, leaders need to shake the team out of this plateau by creating what we call positive turbulence. This means making changes that question set ways, introduce external elements that break familiarity and openly address weaknesses or bad habits. It could mean resting a star player, raising the bar on fitness and fielding by picking young guns who make everyone else look slow, getting a different coach who introduces stringent work ethic norms, getting a consultant who takes an external, neutral view of things. It ensures that teams are ready for change should it hit them suddenly. In fact sometimes the environment forces change upon organisations but in case that does not happen, organisations need to be proactive in getting teams ready for change as and when it happens. Teams can get sluggish and complacent when not challenged and that's a surefire recipe for the beginning of the end. As Sunil Lulla says, 'Nobody can take pole position for granted.'[9] No wonder we find a number of established companies scouting for people with experience of working in start-ups. Another form of positive turbulence, maybe.

In fact, Nitin Paranjpe believes that in the FMCG sector ('and remember, the 'F' in FMCG stands for fast', he says), like in T20 cricket or even a game of table tennis, you need to have your eye on the ball at all times. 'The price you pay for even a momentary lapse can be significant,' he warns.

Ricky Ponting, Australia's cricketing legend but an unsuccessful captain on the subcontinent, wrote similarly after a lost Test match 'The little things, single sessions, opportunities not taken can quickly change a game in India. That partnership (for the ninth wicket between V. V. S. Laxman and Ishant Sharma at Mohali in 2010) not only cost us the game, it has cost us any chance of winning the series.'

So, as you can see, winning is brilliant, worth dreaming about, but only sustainable if you remember not to take your eyes off the ball.

Managing Success

- Success must be analysed with the same rigour as failure.

- Success is in the context of time, space and scale.

- Keep what still works and discard the rest.

- Managing success is as difficult as achieving it.

- Winning comes with side-effects: ego, over-confidence, complacency.

- The Disease of Me can lead to The Defeat of Us.

- Chronic winners need to guard against satisfactory underperformance.

- Adversity separates champions from challengers.

Learning While Losing

Some failure in life is inevitable. It is impossible to live without failing in something unless you live so cautiously that you might as well have never lived at all. In which case, you failed by default.

—J. K. Rowling

Bookstores are well-stocked with success stories about Google, Yahoo, Coke or Nike. There are many pages on what Jack Welch did right to create a winning team or how Richard Branson managed to build an empire or why Infosys became a success. This might lead you to believe that it is only the successful who can tell you anything worthwhile and that failures, big and small must only head towards the bin and don't even deserve another look. Of course, you feel motivated when you learn from the stars but remember they don't always make the best teachers because, among other reasons, they seem to have the ability to execute even the trickiest of plans and, as mentioned elsewhere in this book, don't always seem to understand why others cannot!

Those wounded and vanquished in warfare not only have scars to display, but with each scar comes a story and a lesson: of what not to do, of errors of judgement, of assumptions that were horribly wrong. Invaluable insights are gained on all that can go wrong and what setbacks can do to otherwise competent teams. It also tells you about how people behave under the pressure of a loss and why some teams recover while others find the burden of failure too heavy to bear.

Failure: An Invaluable Teacher

In India, people are very afraid of failing. In the US, people fail and move on. Here, you try to find ten reasons why you failed, everything except 'you'. In the US, failure is like a badge of honour. Oh, you have been to the war, you have been shot, you must have been a good soldier! India has to develop that culture.

—Dr. Gururaj Deshpande,
Co-Founder, Sycamore Networks[1]

In fact, our attitude to failure, to a setback, tells us a great deal about ourselves, our organisations, and our culture. In India for example, we tend to look at failure as a kind of death, a hauntingly sad tune that must play throughout our lives. The moment a player is dropped from the national team, the newspapers term him a 'Test discard', a terribly insensitive word. He is ignored at airports and stands alone in gatherings.

It is almost as if someone from the flock has strayed and must be made to stand in a corner henceforth. This leads to a fear of failure, which, as we know, is the fastest way to actually get there.

It needn't be like that though. A failure can be a friend for it can tell you where you are fallible, allow you to tighten your game, improve your career. The more mistakes you make, the more you learn about yourself and your ability and consequently, the better you can become. A friend of ours, outstanding at software and logic, argued therefore, that the person who only makes mistakes must be the most knowledgeable. Luckily, mathematical conclusions are not always the most enlightening but it is indeed true that if you are willing to learn from your mistakes you become a better player, a better manager and are of greater value to your side.

The Australian cricketer Michael Clarke was dropped in 2005, a year after an outstanding debut in international cricket. In most places, it would have been viewed as a major setback, but interestingly that very day Mark Waugh said, 'I said he'd be a captain in years to come and I still think he will be … he's got a great cricket brain. It's certainly not the end of the world for Michael Clarke, he's just got to get back and enjoy himself.'

Darren Lehmann wrote in *The Daily Telegraph* that Clarke's sacking would make him a better player, just as it did for the Waugh brothers. 'It's not the worst thing that can happen. He'll come back a better player. All good players go through it. They've obviously made the call he needs to go away and make runs and he'll do that on his ear. He'll be back, no doubt about it.'

These were statements of faith no doubt but also pointers that you must experience the rough with the smooth. Much later Clarke agreed, 'As much as you hate getting dropped, it certainly gave me some time to re-assess.' As has been mentioned later in this chapter, initial failures can be like potholes on a road; in course of time you know where they are and can avoid them easily. By late 2006, Clarke had scored back-to-back centuries in an Ashes series, was made vice-captain of the team and thereafter appointed captain of the T20 side and eventually ended up as a pretty successful Australian captain and the International Cricket Council Player of the Year for 2013.

Brendon McCullum, one of New Zealand's finest captains and, towards the end of his career, a fine ambassador for cricket, talked very candidly in his MCC Spirit of Cricket Lecture in June 2016, about how being bowled out for 45 on the first morning of a test match in Cape Town completely changed the way they looked at themselves. '… we just spoke from our hearts; about who we were as a team and how we were perceived by the public. It was agreed that we were seen as arrogant, emotional, distant, up-ourselves and uninterested in our followers. The environment that the younger players were being welcomed into was really poor—there was a very traditional hierarchy, where senior players ruled the roost. Ultimately, we concluded that individually and collectively we lacked character. The key for all of us was the team had no 'soul'. We were full of bluster and soft as putty. It was the first time I had really stopped to consider this in eleven years of international cricket.'

It is an amazing admission to make but it is pertinent to realise too that in a shattering performance lay the seeds of some amazing cricket later. But if they hadn't looked failure in the eye, nothing would have changed.

It's probably predictable that most people and teams would like to take credit for success. Credit is rarely given to the role that the external environment plays in that success. All industry benchmarks come only from successes. Failure on the other hand is the orphan that organisations and individuals are both too shy and too scared to talk about. That is the reason why success stories are so well-documented while failure is strictly limited to post- mortems within the organisation. While the truth is that failure in fact gets analysed a lot more than success, it is often with the intention of putting the blame on persons, processes or even the environment or market conditions, rather than learning from it.

Like you can learn from your own failure, you could learn from the failure of others as well. That is if they are open to sharing it honestly and are encouraged by the organization to do so without the blame game. Subroto Bagchi believes that failure is a rich thing but it's rich provided that there is a harvesting methodology. 'There is a harvest waiting at the end of the failure,' he says. 'Mind Tree, you know is a software company and software companies are full of projects. Sometimes, projects fail and typically people talk about post-mortem. Let's do a post-mortem. When I came in, I said look don't talk about a post-mortem, it's so gory. Let's talk about a post-harvest review. After every major project, successful or otherwise, let's do a post-harvest review. For every major crisis that we have gone through or failed through there is a book and the book then is used to teach future generation of people who come into the organisation. It teaches them two interesting things. It teaches them how not to repeat those mistakes, but more importantly teaches them a big thing and that is, the failure is ok. So people feel safe in the organisation. When they feel safe that failure is an ally, that failure will not bring personal penalization, and then they are willing to take bigger steps forward.'[2]

Rahul Dravid often talks about the number of times leading players like him and Sachin Tendulkar have failed. If 50 is a benchmark for success, and that is a batting average that the best aspire to have, then between them they managed it 218 times; out of 615 innings. So, admittedly, by a fairly high bar set, they failed 397 times. And yet, they are regarded as legends and that is because they made the good times count. Life isn't measured a failure at a time but over a career and the 218 successes counted for much more than the 397 failures!

After a good spell playing for India, Ravichandran

Ashwin was left out of the Indian team for the first test in Adelaide in Australia in late 2014. He says it caused him to look at himself closely, analyse his game and see what he could do better or, maybe, what he was doing wrong. The introspection lead to one of his most successful phases. And it happened because he, like other successful people, used failure as a stepping stone, to become tougher rather than moan about being victimized and looking for reasons that mollify you but do no good.

I've missed more than 9000 shots in my career. I've lost almost 300 games. Twenty-six times I've been trusted to take the game winning shot and missed. I've failed over and over and over again in my life. And that is why I succeed.

—Michael Jordan[3]

When are Teams At Risk?

It is entirely possible to lose because of external causes and reasons beyond your control. You might for example, lose the toss or there might be a storm, or lots of dew in the second half of the game.

In business terms, the recession for example, had little to do with your own effort or capability. If you are in a business that is affected by government policy or regulations, a sudden and unexpected change in policy, like demonetization or Brexit, could ruin your fortunes; a tax holiday on manufacturing might be removed or entry loads on mutual funds could be dropped. A change in market conditions could dramatically alter your cost calculations and negate your competitive edge. You could even be up against a competitor who has an inherent cost, scale or sourcing advantage over you. In the mid-eighties the Australians had to cope with losing players to rebel tours, in addition to the retirement of stars. State teams in India lost the cream of their talent to the now-defunct rebel Indian Cricket League. Technology might make your product obsolete faster than you thought it would. However, these instances are relatively rare and more often than not, the performance of a team depends on its own talent, attitude and effort.

Around 1992-93, the Indian economy embraced liberalisation and there were sweeping changes in all areas of business. That era witnessed the demise of several top brands and leading business houses that could not cope with the changes and play with new rules. Some of them had got so used to running their businesses a certain way that when many sectors got privatized and more competition came in, they simply wound up and disappeared. Who had ever imagined that brands like HMT, Premier Padmini, or EC TV would one day be history?

Try this exercise. List the top companies in India in 1990 and then again in 2000, and see how much the two have in common. Of course, many of the new entrants would be from new sectors like IT and Telecom, but many of the older brands would be fairly low down in the list for 2000 or may even have ceased to exist.

This happened with a lot of public sector brands that found out that dealing with a consumer, or reaching out to him was something they had never needed to do. Interestingly it happened with some categories of imported products too as the quality of Indian brands improved. This arrival of the consumer, and the choice he now had was a defining era in Indian business. All along, the consumer only had a handful of brands to choose from and nowhere to go to if they didn't deliver on quality. Now switching brands was easy, as was rejecting brands, whether the issue was buying an air ticket, a car or choosing a phone company of choice. Companies that didn't adapt to this change declined rapidly. MTNL and Indian Airlines adapted reasonably but HMT, Premier Padmini, ITDC and many others did not.

So why do some teams go into a slump? Each team has certain assets, be it products or people that deliver results, like fast bowlers for the West Indies in the seventies and eighties, or scooters for Bajaj Auto. They were the star performers. While they delivered, the team won. The team depended heavily on them and probably never imagined life without them. The West Indies took the fast bowlers for granted and did little to ensure their steady supply. Once the generation of Roberts, Holding, Marshall, Garner, Croft and the rest was gone, the West Indian team was a pale shadow of its former self. The likes of Ambrose, Walsh and Bishop kept the flag flying briefly but it was the dance of death rather than the sighting of dawn. The West Indies failed to build a supply chain when the going was good.

Overdependence on stars can also lull the rest of the team into underperformance. It's easy to believe that if you have a Tendulkar or a Jordan or a Kohli in your team it is their job to lead the team to victory as they do so often. Stars fade or retire, sometimes cruelly at one go, as did Lillee, Marsh and Greg Chappell or later, Warne, McGrath, Gilchrist and Hayden. Tendulkar, Dravid, Ganguly and Kumble were also of the same vintage. Teams must anticipate this inevitable development and prepare for succession well in time. Also, from time to time, it's a good idea to rest the stars and test the rest. This empowers the whole team and makes them believe that any one of them can take the team to victory, especially if the star fails on a big day.

In one of the finest innings played on Indian soil, Tendulkar was battling away with a bad back against a strong Pakistan team at Chennai in 1999. He was eventually out 17 short of the target and India lost by 12 runs. Many years later, we asked Wasim Akram, then captain of the Pakistan team, about his thoughts during such a tense match. 'I knew that if we got Tendulkar out we would win the game even if only three were needed to win. I knew India would lose the game in the dressing room itself the moment he was out.' An overwhelmingly big star can win games but is not always good for the development of others if they are not empowered.

Phil Jackson, who achieved as much success with the Los Angeles Lakers as he did with the Chicago Bulls in the mid-nineties, has written (in his book *Sacred Hoops*) about the effect of having Michael Jordan in the team. Jordan assumed he had to win the game for his team but sadly, so did his team mates. In a crunch situation, there was only one man the team could turn to, which of course was great news for the opposition. Until everyone else on the team was empowered to win, which was a subsequent approach followed with great success including back-to-back NBA championships, Jordan scored more points than anyone else but the Bulls didn't win anything. Like Tendulkar and India, they had the best player in the world with them but it did little for the team.

Businesses too can become overly dependent on large clients or suppliers, or indeed, even single brands, leaving them in a vulnerable position. While displaying key clients or preferred suppliers, companies need to keep their dependence on them at the back of their minds. Advertising agencies have gone under when large accounts have moved away from them. ITC's successful diversification into hotels and FMCG products to reduce dependence on the cigarette business is a great case study.

Tata-AIG Insurance relied on one institutional seller for more than 40 per cent of their sales. Then at the height of the recession in the west, that institutional seller aligned with someone else to sell its own insurance products. Faced with a forty per cent drop in a hugely competitive market, Tata AIG had to act quickly to build other distribution streams. They managed to do it but they had to struggle really hard for it. In doing so, they showed that sometimes the exit of a star can have a hugely positive effect on team spirit. Seemingly ordinary players can step up and display qualities that weren't expected of them; collectively they can discover tremendous strength. This is something that star dependent companies and teams should think about.

Bajaj Auto, one of the leading two-wheeler manufacturers from the sixties right until the eighties, assumed that a steady supply of consumers were waiting to buy their scooters. After all, they once had a ten-year-long waiting list and owning a Bajaj Chetak or a Bajaj Super was almost a status symbol. When consumers moved from scooters to more fuel-efficient motorcycles, suddenly the product offering was no longer relevant. Given these circumstances, it took Bajaj quite a while to regain its past glory, even partially.

We have seen how Colgate became stronger after Pepsodent and Close-Up flanked them; it woke them up from a feeling that they were invincible. Nestle had to suddenly live with the fact that their biggest earner, Maggi, had to be taken off the shelves. There was little they could do about one of the most powerful FMCG brands but it returned, if anything, an even more powerful brand.

A team caught up in success sometimes fails to see the world changing. That is what happened with Indian hockey which was oblivious to the fact that the world was moving from natural grass to artificial turf which requires different skills from players. In 1975 India won the World Cup; by 1976 at the Montreal Olympics they ranked at number 7; by 1986 they had finished last at the World Cup. In 2010, the hockey team failed to qualify for the Olympics altogether. India didn't change with the times, didn't get the right players and the right coaches and consequently lived in a time-warp. By the time India embraced modernity, it had to be claw its way back; where once it ruled the game it had to learn from those it had taught. The journey back has been long.

England's cricket team discovered that too in 2015 when they went to play the World Cup in Australia. It was seven years since the IPL, there have been five T20 World Cups, many leagues had sprouted around the world, bats had ballooned in size, rules had been tinkered with and hitherto unimagined scores were being put up. The game had changed. It was no longer a 50-over game as people knew it to be, it was almost a longer version of a T20 match. Attitudes and techniques had changed but England tended to sneer at change. Because of a closed system, the changes in the game around had largely passed them by. At the 2015 World Cup, England looked dated. In their survival match, Bangladesh looked more modern, more in with the times. England slumped to almost inevitable defeat and left the World Cup early.

But at least, somebody was watching. The embarrassing defeat forced a rethink, windows to the world were opened, more contemporary people appointed and limited overs cricket was looked upon as an equal partner to Test cricket. The change was almost immediate.

India at hockey and England at limited-overs cricket are great examples of traditional powers ignoring the winds of change through laziness or arrogance or whatever and having to taste defeat to jolt them back into modernity. You don't want to do that if you are a brand, or an individual performer. In this case, defeat forced teams to become relevant again but good brands, good artistes, smart companies don't wait for defeat to remind them of where they should be.

It can happen with filmmakers too when they struggle to get out of a comfortable but increasingly irrelevant style. Ad-film makers who make commercials for youth must always keep an eye on a changing world and must ensure that they have more contemporary people on their staff so that their style and use of talent remains relevant.

'Unlike in the US, we don't believe in the experimental model and are fatalistic about failure, instead of learning from it,' thinks Sunil Lulla.[4] Few companies and brands manage comebacks. He cites the examples of Star TV, Zee TV along with Amitabh Bachchan and Aamir Khan as media brands that managed to reinvent themselves. Bachchan, the brand gets the vote of most CEOs. As Sandip Das says with a smile, 'He may not be surrounded by girls any more but he has remained relevant.'[5]

New entrants can be your windows to the outside world. That is why Neeraj Garg believes that a stable team has the highest percentage of under-performers.

They reach a steady state and become exceedingly inward looking. Teams that do not have a fresh infusion of talent from time to time lose the alertness that is required in order to keep an eye on what is happening in the outside world. Even successful marketing teams can become large and unwieldy and end up lumbering along unable to move swiftly enough to react to change.

P. Gopi Chand, winner of the All-England badminton tournament and star coach to players like Saina Nehwal, and P.V. Sindhu, when asked why our women players of an earlier era who looked so promising in the initial rounds didn't make it to the finals or semis, said 'Because they were well-coached!' That might seem like a strange and unusual remark to make but he went on to explain that when players indulge in text-book play, there is no element of surprise in their game. They know exactly what they will do in a given situation but sadly, so does their opponent. Predictability can prove to be a weakness in marketing warfare as well.

Another interesting paradox is that a team full of winners can sometimes lose. In 2005, when it appeared that the mighty Australians were unstoppable, especially at home, an all-stars World XI was created to take them on. With no time to gel and with little in common to bond them together, they were no match for the well-oiled juggernaut, losing by huge margins amidst a media frenzy. Apart from not bonding, the other problem with having too many stars in the team is that each of them comes with an ego of matching size and sometimes a personal agenda. A team of champions pulling in different directions can't become a champion team whereas a team pulling together is better than the sum of its parts. The Australians, in their prime, often said they believed they were playing 12 versus 11, with their team spirit being the twelfth player.

Signs of Losing

So if a team is on its way downhill, are there signs that you can pick up? Are there symptoms that teams need to look out for? While every business will have some of its own to add to the list, there are some things they have in common. We have already discussed overdependence on stars. Another one is the reluctance of teams to accept collective responsibility for failure. Instead, they make an individual or some group or department the fall guys and pin the blame on them. Often, losses come during tough situations and one of the signs of a good and united team is that a number of people rise to the occasion; they are willing to put their reputations on the block and to take risks. In losing teams, members don't want to take decisions; they maintain the status quo even if it is doomed and would rather fail than be blamed. In tough situations, losers like to duck. They feign injury or report sick so that they can avoid facing the challenge.

Many years ago, India had an opening batsman who looked at the pitch on the morning of the game and always came back shaking his head, talking of how much bounce it had, or how lively it would be. He was setting the scene for a potential failure, almost laying the ground for it. Another batsman, who had done well in the build-up to a Test match in Perth, was told that as a result, he would be playing the Test on what was then the fastest pitch in the world. On the morning of the game he hobbled up to the team bus and complained to the captain of a stiff back! The captain saw through it very quickly and realizing that a reluctant player was not much good, told the vice-captain to inform one of the substitutes that he was playing instead. Now normally, playing for your country should be a matter of great honour, but the substitute, when told the good news, instead of being excited responded with a 'Me? Why?' He had seen the pitch too and realized that he didn't have much of a chance against top fast bowlers on a really quick pitch. Both players felt that it was better to sit out, to duck a game, rather than confront failure. It was never seen as a challenge, only as an opportunity to fail.

The story is also told of an Indian fast bowler who, on being presented with a flat deck where the bowlers were, effectively defanged, opted out claiming he was injured. As it turned out, the fast bowlers got a pasting in that match and at the end of the day were greeted by the man who had missed the game saying '*Dekha, yahan na khelna hi uchit tha!*' ('See, I told you, not playing was the clever thing to do.') Great strategy, one of the other players in earshot added, 'Don't play, fastest way to get to 400 wickets!'

There are many who quit at the slightest inkling of a difficult time ahead. 'But what you need to overcome tough times is perseverance,' says Sanjay Purohit. 'There is absolutely no running away from a tough time. I have had a very intelligent person, IIT / IIM graduate who continuously skipped jobs as soon as the going got tough. As a result of which his cycle of learning during those tough times was completely inadequate and finally how many times can you flip from one place to another to another? Tough times really give you a great opportunity to hang in there, persevere. It tests you in many ways, it brings out aspects that you perhaps didn't know existed in you yourself and then you complete the cycle of learning. In good times, you don't learn. It's in tough times that you learn not only about your business and what you need to do well but about yourself,' he adds.[6] Interestingly, Sanjay also recommends a thick skin and the ability to face the brutal reality as essentials during tough times. As does the actor Anil Kapoor who has had a longer career than most.

Jerry Rao says that a common sense of purpose keeps good teams focused on winning. Their attention is devoted to the market and to competition. Losing teams focus on internal structures, designations, perks, money and related such themes. Togo's footballers refused to play their group matches at the 2006 World Cup over pay disputes and only relented after FIFA warned them of the consequences. At the 2003 Cricket World Cup in South Africa, a number of the Pakistani players were focused on individual records and there was no mention of a collective desire to win the event. The England cricket captain Nasser Hussain had to spend more time understanding the political situation in Harare than getting his team to play. All attention was focused on the politics around Zimbabwe and when England eventually agreed to play there, they just weren't competitive enough. We are often told by young managers when we present *The Winning Way* to them that life is eventually about the 'package' and the 'package' has to be attractive because of the pressure of EMIs. It is unlikely you will get tougher if at the first sign of a challenge, you look for a bigger package!

It is easy for teams that are doing well to share a sense of camaraderie. It is during tough times, when teams get stretched, that team spirit gets tested. That is when players become insecure and begin to guard their turf. Is it really true then that team spirit leads to success? Or is success the fragile glue that helps hold teams together? A team culture that doesn't just punish a poor result but also acknowledges effort, one where failure is viewed as an avoidable yet rich learning experience is symbolic of a healthy team—one that is adequately equipped to handle difficult situations.

Sometimes teams that are doing pretty well can suddenly lose a couple of games and start doubting themselves. However, a dip in performance does not mean that a team has lost its inherent ability to perform and become worthless. The first casualty that hits teams when they do badly is their self-belief. They start doubting their ability and question their strategies thus far. Their confidence takes a beating, which leads to more defeats, and this signals the beginning of the downward spiral. This is what happened with the Indian cricket team's performances overseas in the nineties. After a few losses, the players stopped believing that they could win and like all self-fulfilling prophecies, it came true again and again.

Ajinkya Rahane seems to have the perfect antidote for self-doubt. Since an idle mind is a devil's workshop, whenever Rahane faces a low period he tries to keep himself very busy to prevent negative thoughts from entering his mind. Rahane, like his role model Dravid is a serious student of the game and a great believer in self-awareness as a key to success. When going through a difficult patch, Virendra Sehwag recommends revisiting the good times. He used to play videos of the times he had done well in order to reinforce his self-belief. He routinely whistled Hindi film songs or sang bhajans to free his mind of unwanted thoughts!

Turning Things Around

To break this cycle, along with improving performance, it is critical to rebuild the confidence of the team. They need to realize that being included in the team means that they are good and that they cannot suddenly become bad overnight; that the cliché 'form is temporary, class is permanent' is actually true. This is the job of the leader for he has the most important role to play in the turnaround.

In sport, the opposition understands this and that is why they often target the leader. They realize that if the leader has lost faith, or is struggling with his own form, he will not be in the best position to demand performance from the others. In fact on *Masterstrokes*, Sourav Ganguly highlighted this situation. 'You need to separate the two roles, as a player and as a captain. If you allow them to merge, your captaincy will deteriorate.'

One way of overcoming this seeming lack of self-belief is for teams to celebrate even small wins to remind them that they can win and that it is the path to breaking the downward spiral. Niall Booker is a big supporter of celebrating even small wins when a team is down. He says the three most important reasons for this are, that the team develops a winning habit, it builds confidence and wins attract talent since everyone loves to work with a winning team. During testing times, leaders often take risks. When they can pull off these risks, the team starts backing the leader for his courage. 'A good example for me was when I was bringing about change in our India business (HSBC). We got the opportunity to purchase around 15-20 per cent of what was then known as UTI Bank (now Axis Bank). Doing this transaction showed we could act quickly, move differently from our competitors and, importantly, be a catalyst for change.

It sent a very positive message throughout the company, especially around the fact that the leader was courageous and could get things done,' remembers Booker.[7]

When Australia arrived in England for the 2005 Ashes, nobody gave the home team a chance, not even England supporters. Very early on in the tour, the teams played a T20 international and the English, in a departure from routine, came hard at the Aussies; they bowled fast and short and discovered that the Aussies could be vulnerable too. The confidence that a small win generated took them through the Ashes. At various times, players stood up and performed with gusto. For the first time in eighteen years, they beat Australia and famously went on to win the Ashes. It was a huge success, but it began with a small win.

A team may be anxious to turn things around as fast as possible but performance does not improve overnight, especially if the defects have been allowed to build up over a period of time. Everyone, including the leader, must be patient. Sandip Das believes, 'When the times are good, stretch them. But when the times are bad, stick to the basics and be honest with yourself.'[9] Batsmen talk about playing in the 'V' with a straight bat, when they are struggling. Once the confidence returns they can get back to playing other shots. So even in tough times, there are things that you can do well. It is important not to let what you cannot do interfere with what you can.

Don't let what you cannot do interfere with what you can. It's a philosophy that we believe in very strongly and one that we find works differently but equally well for most people. Paddy Upton believes that it is more important to focus on your own strengths rather than try and target the weaknesses of your opponents. He talks of his time on the coaching staff of South Africa and how the discussion, based on statistics and analytics, revolved around bowling wide yorkers to M. S. Dhoni to keep him quiet and prevent him from playing big shots. As they were walking back post the meeting Upton asked the bowler if he was confident of bowling wide yorkers and was surprised to get a 'no' in return. 'I don't bowl them too well!' he was told and sure as ever, the attempt backfired in the game.[8] Some time later, Upton was back as coach of the Rajasthan Royals and they were playing against the Chennai Super Kings. Again, analytics suggested that the way to restrain Dhoni was to bowl wide yorkers. The bowler now given the responsibility said, 'I am not very good at it, I am not confident enough, but what I can do is to bowl fast into his rib cage. He can at best fend it away for a single and I'll have him at the other end. He can't win the game from there!' As it turned out, by not letting what the bowler couldn't do come in the way of what he could actually do, the Royals found a way of countering Dhoni.

HR managers are also talking of newer ways to look at performance management where leaders are encouraged to have conversations with their team members about their strengths and how they together can best exploit them to the advantage of the team. This is a far cry from the dreaded annual appraisal where only weaknesses, now politely labelled 'developmental needs' are pointed out. Good teams would rather focus and build on strengths than make excuses.

On the other hand, teams or individuals that have acquired a negative or a defeatist mindset tend to focus on things they cannot do. They will spend a lot of time talking about a bowler they cannot pick, about a winger they cannot mark, about competition getting raw materials at much cheaper rates and other such grievances. Indian banks talk about budgets that MNC banks have while the MNC banks complain they can't compete because they can't open as many branches. So too in the pharma industry where multinationals say they are bound by ethics (which, by inference, suggests Indian companies are not!) while Indian companies say multinationals have higher budgets. Young fast bowlers might start moaning about the fact that they cannot bowl at 150 kmph, or a spinner can worry that he doesn't turn the ball enough, or a full-back can keep thinking he isn't tall enough to counter the crosses from the right wing. If there is nothing you can do about it, there is no point worrying about it. Good teams and good players think about what they can do, about how they can get better at what they do, about things that are in their control. If, for example, an ice cream company cannot get milk as cheap as Amul does, instead of giving up on the product, they could focus on new flavours, on a better retail experience, or better packaging maybe. A bowler who cannot bowl at 150 kmph can, as an alternative, move the ball both ways at a fairly sharp 135 kmph. There is always something you can do. Good teams are patient, they keep chipping away at it, and they get rid of the defects one by one. More often than not, for them the tide will turn.

Resilience, the ability to bounce back and remain optimistic even when the chips are down is seen to be a very valuable attribute in today's VUCA world. While this world offers incredible opportunities for most, it also leaves businesses vulnerable to disruption. It requires companies to be watchful and vigilant at all times. No one can take success for granted any more. You win some, you lose some but you need to remain positive and keep going. Abhinav Bindra echoes this same need to be resilient when he says, 'I don't think of not winning as failure. I don't consider not achieving what you set out to achieve as failure. It's just something that didn't happen. What I consider failure is if you give up.'[9]

Often, organisations condemn the efforts of the team when the desired results are not achieved. Sometimes this happens in the process of trying something new. Needless to say, every experiment and every innovation comes with a risk, even though it may appear only in the fine print. If calculated risks are not taken, the team could stop growing. Jerry Rao points out that there is a saying in banking circles, 'You don't get a promotion till you have made a few bad loans.'[10] While failure is not fatal, over-analysis of failure kills risk-taking and that can eventually prove fatal. India discovered that when they over-analysed the Sri Lankan mystery bowler Ajantha Mendis initially. Dhoni's advice to the team was to just go out and bat aggressively without worrying too much. That worked and the Indian team found out that Mendis wasn't as big a threat as they had made him out to be.

Technology-based products are launched and marketed very differently from let's say FMCG brands. Traditionally brands were subjected to all kinds of market research, then test-marketed, piloted and then launched country-wide. Product limitations were frowned upon. While launching tech products like mobile phones, speed is of the essence. Consumers too are happy to use versions or different models with different features. Products are not expected to be used long-term with people upgrading their phones every couple of years if not months. Models are launched without too much fanfare or expense. If they catch on, well and good. Otherwise they are quietly withdrawn. As one CEO put it, 'There's nothing like success or failure anymore, only feedback.'

The key to turning things around is positivity and the conviction that things will get better soon enough. In any team, there are always those who have faith in the team's ability and remain optimistic that the dark clouds will pass. At the same time, there are also cynics who are quite happy to run down their own team. On *Masterstrokes*, Rahul Dravid talked about the team being like a pot, from which some take out and some put in. A team in which more people contribute is a more positive team.

Sadly, in a bad patch there are more demands to take out of the pot. The team needs to rally around the optimists (who are also generally the people who are doing better than the others) and the cynics need to be sidelined. It's true of individuals as well. Ricky Ponting speaks of the time when he was a little low on confidence after having failed to get runs in a few innings. He said he spent as much time as possible with Mark Waugh who was in good form and was very positive about everything.

India's badminton star Pullela Gopi Chand on his march towards the All England title in 2001 ran into numerous cynics who told him that the Chinese hit too hard and jumped too high, that they could not be beaten and that even if he scored seven points against them instead of four, it would still qualify as a big achievement. Gopi didn't believe there was much difference between losing after scoring seven points or losing after scoring four. He said that he believed he could win and always surrounded himself with positive people who told him he could make it. He said he didn't have specific plans on how to beat the Chinese, just the faith that if he played his game well enough consistently he could win. As it turned out, he beat a Chinese player in the semi-final and one in the final. It was a historic moment in Indian sport.

In the first year of the IPL, the Deccan Chargers were at the bottom of the table. An already disillusioned team got engulfed in rumours that the owners wanted to sell off their stake. The second season of IPL saw a new captain in Adam Gilchrist. He led by example and infused positivity into the team. In a single year he managed to create a turnaround and Deccan Chargers won the tournament in 2009. It is always a challenge to lead a motley, heterogeneous team as in the IPL. The younger members of Rajasthan Royals who won the first season of the IPL credited their captain Shane Warne who always advised them to look ahead and forget about what happened before or to think of what might have been. Those who allow themselves to get caught in the burden of past failure find it difficult to pick themselves up again.

Today's athletes and managers are lucky to have a better support system than earlier, with coaches, mentors, buddies etc. being available to help and guide them. Earlier players feared that if they voiced their anxieties or fears to captains, coaches or even selectors, they would hold their weaknesses against them. Now there are personal coaches and foundations like Olympic Gold Quest or the Go Sports Foundation or the Jindal Sports Foundation whom players can trust to support them without the earlier apprehensions. 'Trust is the key for building rapport with the athletes and getting the best out of them. Without mutual trust, it will be very hard to support the athletes because then you will not even learn about the exact problems they are facing let alone being able to solve them,' says Viren Rasquinha, former hockey player and now CEO, Olympic Gold Quest.[11]

Actually, a small loss often does the team some good. It is a wake-up call to teams who tend to take winning for granted. It can also act as a gentle nudge to purge, to remove flab, to reassess the team's assets and liabilities and to renew their commitment to the common goal. Chronic winners may not always be battle-ready and could be taken by surprise when sudden changes occur. Thus, small losses or challenges actually keep teams on their toes and prepare them for whatever the situation demands. We often talk about how good teams can emerge stronger after defeat because they now know where they are vulnerable. After the West Indies lost to India in the final of the 1983 World Cup, they returned to blank India out in the series that followed and then dominated world cricket like never before. Australia surprisingly lost the Ashes to England in 2005 in an era when they didn't know what defeat meant. In the next eighteen months, they had won the Champions Trophy, demolished England 5-0 at home and retained the World Cup without being challenged.

In fact, leaders respect people who have managed turnarounds, who have clawed their way out of difficult situations. Adversity toughens up people, makes them dig deep into their resources and helps them understand their strengths and their limits. Sandy Gordon, an Australian sports psychologist, told us that in the Australian Armed Forces you often don't make it to an elite squadron unless you have failed and come back at some time for it shows resilience and strength. Saugata Gupta says, 'I would rate a person higher if he has either created something or turned something around. That shows character.'[12]

During their great run in the first edition of the IPL, the Rajasthan Royals suddenly lost to a struggling Mumbai Indians team. That night their captain Shane Warne said he wasn't disappointed at all. He thought it was a good time to lose a game so that the team knew that if they dropped their standards they could lose. He thought it would be a great learning experience and could make the team stronger!

So, mistakes are invaluable because they teach you lessons. They are like potholes on the road that you learn to avoid. Mistakes warn you about where you shouldn't be going and what not to do the next time round. Winning is not about not making mistakes, but about how to learn from them and become wiser and stronger. It's not about not getting knocked down but about how fast you can get up and fight again.

Symptoms of Losing Teams

- Bureaucratic; delaying decisions.
- Egos, internal competition, group-ism.
- Getting credit more important than getting the job done.
- Lack of focus, energies spread thin.
- Not enough back-up plans.
- The same few people perform, no new people or ideas.
- Too many or too few processes.
- Crab mentality.
- Blaming others or the environment for failure.
- Weighed down by past failure.

Change

It is not the strongest of the species that survive, nor the most intelligent, but the one most responsive to change.

—Charles Darwin

'If the rate of change on the outside exceeds the rate of change on the inside, the end is near,' wrote Jack Welch.[1] Great line! If your consumers are changing faster than the products you can deliver to them, you run the risk of becoming irrelevant. Cricket might have gone down that path if it had continued to offer only Test cricket to a generation that spends a lot of time and energy comparing the speed of gadgets!

Indeed as we know, England's limited-overs cricket team almost became an illustration of Welch's line through their performance at the ICC World Cup 2015 by putting on a performance that was so dated that it seemed like they were playing in black and white! The rate of change outside England cricket was rapid. Within English cricket the air was static and carried the odour of a bygone era. When they changed, they came back contemporary, exciting and unrecognizable.

Apart from the industrial revolution, the last three decades have probably witnessed more change than ever before. Dhirubhai Ambani's dream of making a phone call cheaper than a post card has come true. We can now get by without ever going to the bank or the ticketing office or even carrying cash. We are transferring money on mobile phones. We are in touch with hundreds of friends on Facebook but can't remember their contact numbers or birthdays. It's a changed life, for better or worse. The world has come closer and yet people have grown apart.

The technological revolution, with its cheap and easy connectivity, has contributed to opening up global opportunities and access to unfamiliar consumer segments. This has changed the balance of power in favour of developing economies. The consumer revolution has been further strengthened by the retail revolution. This has meant changing equations between manufacturers and retailers.

Slowly but steadily, a sports revolution too took root in a country largely seen as a poor, third world nation with no imprint whatsoever on the international sports scene. While cricket is still the only team sport where we count at an international level, at an individual level we have world champions in shooting, boxing, chess, badminton, tennis and wrestling. We now have seeded golfers and athletes and a home-grown kabaddi league has taken off. There is much anticipation surrounding the football league, the hockey league has been a pioneer of sorts and even badminton is paying its players decent money.

Amidst all these changing dynamics, whether or not you can adapt has become a prime determinant of whether or not you can succeed. Over the last few years some have managed to do it well, some struggled but finally settled down, and many others, like Indian hockey, resisted change and eventually lost out. It is only in the last couple of years that this sleeping giant has started showing signs of emerging from its self-induced slumber. In this helter-skelter world, technologies become obsolete quickly, businesses perish rapidly and people become redundant. It's scary and so people have to adapt faster than ever before; where batting for six hours was previously a sign of distinction, you are being asked how many you can score in 20 balls.

Now in his forties, world chess champion Viswanathan Anand finds life challenging. The game has evolved and competition comes from prodigies in their twenties like Magnus Carlsen of Norway. 'You have to ride those changes, new approaches, new ways of playing the game. If you are enthusiastic and keen to learn, that's the main thing,' he says.[2]

Change, Challenges and Comfort Zones

Change is not an enemy, it is merely a challenge to a set way of doing things, a push to get out of your comfort zone and go into unfamiliar territory. We live in a dynamic environment and so, whether it is a change from within or forced upon us from outside, we have to discard old ways of doing things and learn new ways if those are essential to survival. Eventually we discover that change is not the monster we feared it to be. Like bathing under a cold shower, using Twitter, or learning to play the scoop over the wicket-keeper, we get used to it. Change must only be resisted where it invades a person's moral sphere, like in taking or offering a bribe. Old-timers, of course, think slogging everything over mid-wicket or playing the reverse sweep is immoral as well!

Humans, by nature, are creatures of habit. They get comfortable with things they use regularly, whether it is a bus route or a particular type of computer software, or indeed a fielding position, a batting number or a doubles partner! People get accustomed to their workplace and to the people they work with, to a locker room and a training ground. Familiarity breeds comfort. No wonder they get thrown off-balance if there is a change in schedule or job description. Transfers are not always welcome and organisational restructuring is always viewed with suspicion. Tigers in domestic cricket sometimes end up looking like harmless puppies against international competition. Many established Test players initially found it difficult to embrace the T20 format.

During one of our sessions with HSBC, we were told of this outstanding employee who was promoted from the clerical cadre and was told he would now be a manager. His boss was delighted at being able to give him the good news and it came as a bit of a shock to him when he was told the clerk didn't want the promotion and he didn't want to change the comfortable life he had got used to. He didn't want to give up what he had for something he wasn't sure of. He was happy in his zone, like some people who are happy going on a cricket tour but not too keen to play the difficult Tests. Each of us must discover what we want in life. A comfort level and constant progress are enemies arrayed against each other. There is an apocryphal story of an Indian player who confided to his friends that if he hadn't been made to play Tests overseas he might have been able to lengthen his career.

Apart from the fact that change means a disruption of what you are used to and brings a certain sense of discontinuity, there is also a fear of the unfamiliar, like with our clerk from HSBC. As time goes by and you settle down into a routine, you become very secure about a certain way of doing things. Batsmen at number three like the additional five minutes they get to gather their thoughts, check out their kit and to relax. They don't like to get rushed into going out to open the batting within ten minutes of getting off the field. Conversely, openers like the idea of getting on with things rather than sitting around doing nothing for a while. They become edgy and use up all their energy in waiting. Each of them gets used to a certain way of doing things and doesn't like a disruption in routine. However, the test lies in whether you can face it. If you can't, and a fine young kid turns up to take your place, you have nowhere to go. More recently, as India has evolved into the back-office capital of the world, we hear seniors from these firms based in cities like Hyderabad suggest that while opportunities are immense and often global, the local talent (and their families) are still stuck with limited vision and an old-fashioned mindset.

Change May Be Risky But Not Changing Is Riskier

So will you be equally comfortable and successful with a new way? Fear of failure often prevents people from experimenting with anything new. There is also anxiety about adjusting to new people or processes. New technology (which has been the biggest change agent) can be initially very confusing and unnerving. If the older generation, for example (and many of us are either in, or entering that category!), who after great effort have familiarised themselves with some software or the other, is asked to upgrade to something fancier, there is bound to be resistance. Letting go of the past is more difficult than you think. If that past has been fairly successful and rewarding, change becomes even more unwelcome.

In cricket-crazy India, most people are not even aware that it is hockey that is designated as our national sport.

From 1928 to 1956, the Indian men's team remained unbeaten in the Olympics, garnering six gold medals in a row. The Indian team has won a total of eight gold, one silver and two bronze medals in the Olympics. In March 2008, India lost 2-0 to Britain at Santiago, Chile, failing to qualify for the Beijing Olympics, a humiliating 'first' for a country with such a glorious tradition in the game.

It's only now that Indian hockey looks like it has turned the corner. Till a few years ago, Indian hockey was in the news for all the wrong reasons; in-fighting in the Indian Hockey Federation, controversies regarding the hiring and sacking of coaches, unrest among players on issues relating to facilities, wages and other such issues.

The story of Indian hockey in the last three decades is one of refusal to embrace change, leaving too much till too late and not having a process in place even when change was recognised as something that was inevitable. The game that Indians were champions at 50 years ago is not the same as the one that is played today. In those days, hockey was played on grass and the Indian style of wristy shots and pretty moves was perfect for the surface. Europe, home to Astroturf surfaces, was the earliest to move to the artificial surface, about 40 years ago. Even today, countries like Holland and Australia have several times the number of Astroturf grounds as there are in India. It's not as if no attempts have been made to modernise the game in our country. The problem is that attempts that aim only at the top of the pyramid cannot have effects that are either substantial or lasting.

For decades, the hockey establishment was run by politicians, former bureaucrats and retired players, none of whom could really contribute towards better management of the game. Mismanagement, in-fighting and lack of a professional approach turned away potential sponsors and broadcasters from the game. So in spite of having loads of raw talent in the country, and some good coaches in recent times, Indian hockey has to overcome a lot of baggage in facilities and mindsets to regain its lost glory.

If the past is glorious, we tend to keep living there and if the past has been traumatic, we retain those wounds. A few years ago when Dwayne Bravo, the fine West Indies cricketer, was told that the Australians, then undisputed world champions, were in a week-long camp to prepare for the series, he looked bewildered. 'A camp? To play us?' he said. So accustomed had he become to his side losing. What a climb down for the mighty Windies—and yet there it is!

The past impinges on the present, but in sport, as in most things in life, you *must* live in the present. The ball that has baffled you is gone and you are alive to play another. If you keep thinking of that ball, it will cloud your judgement and make it difficult for you to play the next one. You learn from the moment gone by, but you must act in the present.

Organisations that introduce change therefore, often encounter reactions like:

Have we been wrong all this while?

This is how we've always done it!

It's not fair!

The primary response to change, as we can see, is one of uncertainty. A certain amount of apprehension is justified because not all experiments succeed and not all innovations become hits.

Yet—change is something that you cannot avoid or delay beyond a point. Change may be risky, but often, *not* changing could be riskier. Consumers change and so do their tastes. Singers who lip-sync might be okay and the need to acquire a classical base for music might be deemed irrelevant. Swanand Kirkire, the talented, but younger lyricist while in a conversation with the legendary Gulzar saab pointed out that the success of today's songs is no longer determined by the quality of lyrics but on whether the first two lines make for a good ringtone or not. It's not something Swanand was happy about, but there was no escaping the new commercial reality. If you watch old Hindi movies or even recordings of old cricket matches, you realise how slow and boring they now seem. We once tried to get our children to watch *Jaane Bhi Do Yaaro* and found they had lost interest within half-an-hour.

'Was everything as slow then?' they asked. We discovered why, when we went to see the latest edition of *Star Wars*. While to us it seemed like a special-effects showreel, the kids were engrossed! And teenagers today, brought up on superhero movies, might well find those old Star Wars movies to be too slow as well!

Almost inevitably, new generations are unrecognisable from the previous ones and so are their tastes. If you keep your product offering unchanged over the years, it will get rejected, making way for more contemporary products. HUL learnt that and so even a powerful brand like Lifebuoy which was a purely functional carbolic soap in the economy price range, morphed into a pleasant smelling, fairly premium product that came even in a handwash variant.

The Tata Group under Ratan Tata tried to become nimble and dynamic, ready to take on global competition and yet you could see the generation gap in operation when Cyrus Mistry tried to stamp his imprint on the group. As the founders moved out of Infosys, there was similar turmoil.

One has to change with the times. What brought you so far may not necessarily be what will take you forward. Cricket's contemporary product, T20 and a new improved Lifebuoy are good examples of an outside-in approach, looking at what the consumer needs, and changing in keeping with those trends.

The four fast bowler theory brought the West Indies a lot of success but as the quality of the bowlers dipped they failed to find another path. As one of their legends, Michael Holding once said, 'There are no fast bowlers no more ... they merely run in a long way!' By 2010, fifteen years after a dramatic decline, they were bowling more overs with spin and while in the years that followed they found a niche in the instant format of T20 cricket, they had become largely irrelevant in the form that saw them at their greatest—test cricket.

Success therefore needs to be put in context; in the context of time, space and scale—as even Manmohan Desai and Yashraj Films discovered with their lost-and-found or love in Switzerland themes! So you can only fully replicate success *ceteris paribus*. Accordingly, if the circumstances under which you had succeeded have changed, your winning formula will also have to be altered. Not all of it maybe, but after careful consideration and analysis, teams learn to keep what works and discard the rest. The fine balance between continuity and change, like the balance between youth and experience, or freshness and stability, needs to be achieved.

However, it is true that teams get tested during times of change, especially if skills, or attitudes, are deemed irrelevant. When Australia began their remarkable fight back from virtually the bottom of the table in 1985-86, they chose to rebuild keeping attitude first. It didn't matter if you were more skilled, but if your attitude wasn't good enough you had no place. It led to a fair churn, some good players were let go, but attitude became the foundation for the development of an outstanding side. Overnight, if you weren't possessed of attitude, or were unable to adapt, you were redundant. It could happen to any of us; the only thing we are good at might become irrelevant if we don't see the signals ahead.

Positive Turbulence Helps You Stay Ahead of Change

Sometimes, market situations, new technology or new competition can force organisations to change. We might therefore need to cope with change that has been thrust upon us from the outside, as we saw with England's limited-overs cricket team. That is why organisations need to be proactive just to force themselves out of their inertia. When one is used to doing business a certain way and there aren't any challenges to keep you on your toes, it's easy to slack off and not be alert. No surprise then that the worst accidents take place on highways, not on crowded streets. Look at how the good batsmen get out against weak bowling in easy matches.

Also, the greater the mass, the higher the inertia. Large monopolies, especially highly regulated businesses or chronic winners are the perfect profile to exhibit such inertia. Such organisations, we believe, can do with a dose of positive turbulence from time to time. Positive turbulence is change that organisations impose on themselves, without any provocation from the outside, to sharpen their reflexes in their attempts to improve performance. For example, the introduction of Yuvraj Singh and Mohammed Kaif to the Indian cricket team forced the other players to run and dive in the field. They forced positive change on the team and improved the overall standard of fielding to the extent that by 2016, it was as good as any team playing cricket. Younger players saw the impact that some of those from an earlier generation had created and realised that in the modern game, they had no choice but to be supremely fit and fast.

Many corporations too have successfully created positive turbulence. More recently, the pharmaceutical multinational Roche slashed prices on two of their cancer drugs by almost 50 per cent and reintroduced them with different brand names in India. When Roche realized that India had cleared the way for local generic drug-makers they thought they would safeguard their market-share—though at reduced margins, rather than lose it to competition. It was a masterstroke that saw Roche doubling volume on these two drugs.

In sport, probably the most dramatic illustration of how a change in approach every few decades led to a higher and sustained level of performance comes from the high jump. During the 1968 Olympics in Mexico City, most high-jumping champions used the style most popular in those days, called the 'straddle'. Dick Fosbury, not considered a medal contender then, introduced a new style, now popularly referred to as the 'Fosbury Flop'. Like with most innovators, initially he encountered a large number of naysayers. Fosbury has been quoted as saying that the crowds would 'hoot and holler' when he performed his jumps. Fosbury managed to set a new record in Mexico City, jumping 7 feet 4 inches, an inch higher than the next best competitor, Edward Caruthers who used the straddle style. Between 1900 and 1960, the average annual increase in the world high jump record was one-sixth of an inch. Since 1960, it has been one-third of an inch.

Men's High Jump World Record

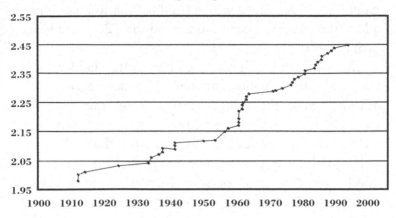

You can see the approach in T20 cricket too where players are no longer intimidated by large run-rates. You will hear people say, almost casually, that this is a '200 run surface'! And so, it will be interesting to see what the next dramatic change in cricket is.

Change is at the centre of growth and expansion. Businesses don't always grow in a linear fashion. While continuity is like the roots of a tree, giving it longevity, change is like the branches that help the tree flourish. How much can a company with a single product grow? Eventually, in order to grow it will have to introduce other products because the tide can go out very fast, as it did with such established products as old-style film cameras (with the arrival of digital cameras and cellphones that took photographs) and compact discs. Or indeed with watches where the need to know the time was fulfilled by the all-encompassing cell-phone! Cricket would have been faced with a similar situation had it not added the one-day international and the T20 game to its product mix.

Even as you climb the corporate ladder, job responsibilities change and new skill sets need to be added. Again, the things that got you this far, like technical expertise, subject knowledge or capacity for hard work, may not be the same qualities that will make you a good leader. For that you will probably need vision, good instinct and great personnel-management qualities.

Mr. Y. M. Deosthalee who has held several CFO positions in the L&T group, but more importantly, someone who has seen a lot of change in the business environment in India points out a subtle, but critical, change in the finance function, for example. Finance professionals tended to be chartered accountants who had grown from the audit and accounts function and so their first instinct to expense was to say no. Their mindset was one of control and compliance. But as Indian businesses grew in the new liberalised environment, finance professionals had to become business enablers. He thought they needed to acquire an MBA mindset rather than a CA mindset and while that may not seem too difficult, it is a huge change in approach. Those that were stuck in control and compliance were perhaps out of place as partners in growing businesses.[3]

Former British Prime Minister Harold Wilson, who probably was witness to far less change than you and me said, 'He who rejects change is the architect of decay.'[4] Today, more than ever before, personal obsolescence is a real danger. When change happens, the effect is as immediate as the change of seasons. It is not something that you can prevent or avoid. It is both inevitable and urgent. The more you delay or resist it, the more time you have lost. It is also a myth that the leader in the team normally leads change. Two of the greatest changes to the limited-overs game came from those playing minor roles.

Before the World Cup of 1996, Sri Lanka were not among the powers of the game but their opening batsmen redefined the way limited-overs cricket would be played. Romesh Kaluwitharana and Sanath Jayasuriya batted aggressively from the word go, making full use of the fielding restrictions in the first 15 overs and making them look like slog overs. In subsequent years, other teams began following the trend that the Sri Lankans had set in 1996. A few years later, a cricketer called Douglas Marillier from Zimbabwe started hopping across to off-stump to scoop full-length balls over short fine leg. Tilakaratne Dilshan modified the 'Marillier' or 'paddle scoop' as it came to be known, hitting the ball straight over the wicket-keeper's head and creating his own 'Dilscoop'—another example of change emerging from the lower echelons.

In fact, today, smaller companies are more agile and nimble and in a far better position to introduce innovation. Sometimes large organizations are simply handicapped by their systems and processes. As Shripad Nadkarni, an old Coke hand and later mentor to the innovative ethnic drinks brand Paper Boat said in an interview, 'Often large companies cannot make a success of new categories such as these. The systems are geared towards high volume, high throughput. That is something in Paper Boat's favour.'[5] If the leader is caught napping, this could mean trouble. Imagine a terrific packaging innovation introduced by a smaller player, along the lines of what Cavin Kare did with sachets in the shampoo market all those years ago. A market-leader who is following the change, not leading it, can be stuck with a whole stock of old packaging before he can copy the new one. 'However, if a giant is the first to introduce the change, just imagine the momentum,' points out Nitin Paranjpe.[6]

Teams that practise positive turbulence can stay ahead of the change. Like hackers who test a company's security systems or Google-staffers who are given time to develop their own projects, maybe the day is not far when companies hire people to see if disruptive change can be beneficial.

Change Needs Ambassadors

So if change is inevitable yet risky, urgently required and yet uncomfortable, how does a leader steer his team through a turbulent phase? How do you ensure that the blueprint of restructuring or reorganisation gets executed well at all levels? Firstly, you must have complete conviction about the plan. If a leader hems and haws over it, there is no chance that the plan will succeed. The next step is to get a buy-in from the entire team. For this to be successful, the leader must almost be an evangelist, for there will be resistance from key stakeholders.

We did a session for a large auto company where the objective was to set ambitious growth targets and the company needed the dealers to change with them to achieve the targets. This meant changing the way showrooms looked and hiring smarter people to service clients, among other things. They ran into a roadblock with the dealers who said that theirs was a time-tested method since they knew each of their customers on a personal level. They were loath to let go of this old-world approach which had worked very well up to a certain point but wasn't practical if the new ambitious sales figures had to be achieved. It required great persuasive skills from the leader to get the critical buy-in!

Another similarly large Chennai-based company faced a very unusual and somewhat amusing challenge. They were in the process of developing a-first-of-its-kind-in-the-world tech-based service platform. They seemed ready to make a grand entry into the global market except that their managers found it challenging to trust people who didn't speak Tamil! Though Tamil is a rich, respected language that served the group well as long as it remained homogeneous, given that the ambition was global in nature, it was inevitable to make English as the working language even if it meant stepping out of the team's comfort zone. Creating the atmosphere for quick and seamless adoption of the global language for doing business became an unexpected leadership priority.

The key to this acceptance of change is in the change initiator addressing the all-important question, 'What's in it for me?' There has to be an exciting and inviting game plan that has to be communicated to the team in the most inspiring fashion. Even so, there will be sceptics who will run down all ideas. There will be some doubters who will need some more convincing. Sometimes, the old guard can feel insecure, as we discovered with an organisation where an expatriate CEO had arrived to drive change. In one of our sessions, we gave them a slightly modified version of the Greg Chappell-Sourav Ganguly situation where an external change agent was trying to bring about drastic change. The younger, more ambitious employees bought into the need for change very easily, while the senior managers resisted it out of insecurity. It was a learning experience for the CEO to see such a clear divide when change was in the air. It helped him address the situation better.

Neeraj Garg believes that organisations must have younger players who will keep the older players aware of changing trends, like Yuvraj and Kaif did with their sliding and diving in the field. There will be the optimists, the enthusiasts, who have to be used as change ambassadors. Change multiplies geometrically if there are enough people with a 'can-do' attitude, which is why the role of the change ambassadors becomes important. This is especially true of large organisations where a changed mission statement might emerge out of a boardroom in Mumbai but will have to be implemented in places like Villupuram and Sonepat.

Often, companies bring in outsiders as change agents since outsiders come with no baggage about the new organisation and bring in a fresh perspective. What they also bring in often, are their own groupies from the old company. There is a fear that an Us versus Them situation can arise, especially during this stage which is fraught with anxiety and uncertainty. You see this in football all the time. For example, when an Italian manager takes over an English team. He brings with him an assistant manager, a trainer, a physiotherapist and the like, and a situation could well develop where the players might say 'Hang on, who is the team? Is it us English or them Italians?'

A time of change comes with several challenges for the team and these are only some of those challenges. A team that makes the changeover successfully and optimistically is likely to make its bonds stronger in the process.

Innovation

Never before in history has innovation offered promise of so much to so many in so short a time.

—Bill Gates

All those years ago, when we were at IIM-Ahmedabad, we had a celebrated Professor of Marketing called Abhinandan Jain. He would spend class after class, make us do version after version of the Stage 1 submission of our Market Research project till we had identified what the problem was. He believed, and rightly so, that till you define the problem accurately, you could not make progress in finding the solution. He had another favourite line that rings true so many years later. The status quo, he would say, can be the solution but only if it is the outcome of rigorous examination. Years later, in a more recent conversation we heard Anand Mahindra echo Prof. Jain's thoughts, 'I think the job of leadership in a company is, whenever an idea comes forward, whenever a solution comes, before you leave that room, before you say okay, this sounds good, and even if that idea sounds like something which is what your mind was hoping for, ask, is there an alternative? To me the core of any kind of innovation is asking, what are the alternatives?'[1]

This examination of the status quo is vital. Often when confronted with a challenge to existing thought, people can go either of two ways. They can latch on to what they know best and talk down impending change or they can jettison the present in a headlong rush to do something different. Both are fraught with danger, especially in these turbulent times.

Challenging the givens is an integral part of innovation. If you need to get better, faster or more accurate, you need to do things differently; change your action, add more strokes or make the training process more efficient. Sport throws up many examples of such change, whether it is the Fosbury Flop, referred to earlier in this book, the 3-point scoring pattern of the Golden State Warriors in the NBA, reverse swing, the *doosra*, the switch-hit ... there are so many.

But, once in a while, someone shakes the very foundation by questioning the basic rules of the game, challenging the assumptions that have shaped the game or the business over several decades. Every sport has its playbook, every sector of business its unwritten givens that are handed down from generation to generation by coaches or industry veterans who define 'the way things are done here'. Starting with the selection and induction program, youngsters are constantly reminded about falling in line and complying with these norms. Till Gen Y arrived, most people were happy blindly following whatever they had been taught. Data and analytics had not arrived on the scene and so 'In India, cricket is religion' meant that it was blasphemous to even argue about where the game was going. The new generation was not a single sport generation unlike their forefathers. They had grown up on a steady dose of European football, Formula 1 racing and even basketball. To win their share of attention, cricket was competing not only with these other sports but also video games and the internet. Gen Y was attracted to entertainment that was fast and furious and result-oriented. Patience and nostalgia, emotions associated with Test cricket and increasingly even with one-day cricket, was not what this generation was all about. Slowly yet steadily, like Levis jeans, cricket had become a dad's brand.

The dramatic arrival of T20 cricket, first in England, then at the World T20 but tellingly so, at the IPL signalled an innovation that was perfect for cricket, almost like a much-needed round of blood transfusion.

T20 emerged out of a customer need identified through market research and it originated, interestingly, in England, a bastion of orthodoxy and the home of test cricket. T20 offered a quick, snappy single evening format of cricket that people could watch after they were home from work. It seems a no-brainer now but it was revolutionary when it was first proposed because the shortest form of the game then was 50 overs, occasionally 40 overs in England. Much like the first World Cup in 1975, the World T20 in South Africa in 2007 was a journey into the unknown. We didn't know it then but when India won it, beating Pakistan in a marketer's dream final, it was to be one of the biggest turning points in cricket, as we knew it. Increasingly, companies and businessmen are talking about disruption and the events of September 24, 2007 were to lay the foundation for one of the biggest disruptions in sport. Most often, it takes an Uber or an AirBnB, players outside the system, to disrupt business models. With T20 you could say, cricket disrupted itself!

Like consumer product offerings, sport must always stay connected to its consumers because there are newer choices everyday. Cricket had started to stagnate a little bit in its offering. Test cricket, this generation's grand allowance to an earlier generation to indulge itself, was already seeing declining viewership in some countries and the 50-over game had just come out of one of the most dreary World Cups ever in 2007. People wanted to watch the top and tail and let go of the middle overs, rather appropriately referring to then as a 'non-aggression pact' between bowler and batsman. In effect, T20 lopped off the middle and gave the spectator the top and tail of a limited overs game. And as the leagues spread all around the world, it did something else. In keeping with what the generation was starting to do with everything else, it offered an 'experience and discard' model of viewing sport. You no longer needed to remember what happened at Chepauk in 1974-75, or Leeds in 2002 or Mumbai in 2004. No. You enjoyed the game as it happened, you sat on the edge of your seat, surfed the unpredictability and left everything behind with the result and moved on.

The real face of disruption though, was to be seen a little over six months later. Actually a bit earlier, when the greatest players in the world were up in the auction and industrialists sat by a table to bid for them. It shook the traditionalists and the outrage, even in a lesser social media era, was substantial. 'Cricketers are being paraded and sold like cattle' was something we heard very often. It was no longer a panel of former cricketers picking the current ones. And so, as you would imagine, there was a bit of box-office involved. A phenomenon, already prevalent in other evolved leagues in the world had arrived in India. 'Can you score runs and take wickets?' was a valid question but so was 'Can you attract people to stadiums? Or can you attend sponsor functions so they can associate with my team?' In the years to come, fine player as he was, Yuvraj Singh's connect with audiences would play as big a role as his cricket, in the enormous valuations he commanded.

Like with all disruption, the arrival of T20 and its flagbearer, the IPL, left a generation of people uncertain of how to tackle the new beast. It went, not just against things they held dear, but also against things that they knew. You see it all the time and you can understand why people hold on to what they know best because they are threatened. That is why it is often said that the influencers in society are often one generation, occasionally two, behind reality. Digital marketing has done that, so has the retail revolution and increasingly, the challenge for middle managers is to stay relevant in rapidly changing times for the tide that brings in change can take them out!

England sneered at the IPL, looked upon it as the worst thing to happen to the game. As we have seen, they looked hopelessly dated at the World Cup of 2015 where many of the semi-finalists had played the IPL and, as we write this, England is making valiant attempts to have its own version of the IPL. It required a change of guard in management to see the reality that the younger players saw but those that controlled them were blind to. We fear that can happen to managers who cannot understand India under 30!

To some extent, this is why 'unlearning' is occupying the mind of leaders of corporate India as much as learning is. And the IPL is a fascinating case study of how unlearning was critical, indeed of how to react to disruption that struck at the very roots of what they had learnt and of how they looked at things. We will present some thoughts on that and it might be a good idea for you to relate those to your businesses and see which part of it you identify with.

As far as T20 was concerned, while changes in technique and shot-making, and as a consequence, in the kind of balls delivered by bowlers, were fairly dramatic, the essential change was in the thought process. When the mind is accepting, changes in execution are inevitable and easier. And as it turns out always, some players made the transition better than others.

When the IPL first started, players prided themselves in not letting the bowler get them out. That is how the likes of Dravid, Kallis and Chanderpaul had been taught the game, that is how they became great players. Their assessment of risk was precise and so they were very good at deciding which balls to play and which to leave. But in a 120-ball game, you couldn't leave too many and so you were forced to play shots that your risk assessment system would have rebelled against. How could they come to terms with the fact that the price they placed on their wicket was not only diluted but that the dilution was welcome and essential? Worse still, their ability to bat for a day-and-a-half was irrelevant. It was actually weighed unfavourably against someone who could find bizarre gaps in a 20-ball innings.

Some adjusted, found new roles for themselves but some others were so ingrained into their set ways that they lost out on the revolution. Rahul Dravid's was an interesting evolution. He decided to open the batting, ensure there were no early wickets lost and at the point where his strike rate could become a liability, he took the price off his wicket. Accepting that it was okay to get out thereafter (in fact, that it would benefit his team sometimes if he got out!) was a giant leap for Dravid as it was for many players who grew up with his cricketing upbringing.

Anil Kumble said that he initially looked upon T20 as easy because he was used to bowling thirty overs in a day and now only had to bowl four. He says he realised quickly that you don't bowl four overs, not even one over but, essentially, one ball at a time. You cannot lull a batsmen into your trap and get him out three overs later because by then someone else would be bowling!

Like Dravid, he made the transition beautifully, but only after he had accepted the colossal change to his thought process.

There is a parallel, we suspect, in manufacturing companies who long prided themselves in making products that lasted for a very long time. The early Nokia phones, for example, were extraordinarily sturdy. But if purchasing trends suggest that consumers are looking for something new all the time and that buying cycles are now no more than 12-18 months long, does it make sense to invest in manufacturing a product that can last much longer? Are cheap, feature-filled mobile phones then, the equivalent of the 'experience and discard' theory mentioned earlier? And the sturdy handsets the equivalent of someone who could bat long hours but whose skill is no longer considered relevant! Older readers who grew up equating Sony with the best in audio and video equipment will recall that Sony faced an identical challenge when Samsung came along.

The idea behind these examples is not to recommend that people take a short-term view of business in times of change but that when disruption is inevitable, you question yourself, your relevance and accept the need to adapt.

As part of the change, players had to get used to being accountable to a different set of people too. For ages, players were held accountable by the selectors, maybe the captain, by the cricket boards at best. Now they were being assessed by people who did the numbers on return on investment. It was a metric that was unheard of in the game but which, as the IPL rolled on, would become a primary tool to assess players and which would determine whether or not a contract was renewed. A lot of players who had tended to look down on the people in suits found it very difficult to reconcile to the fact that they were in fact the new bosses.

For many years, every cricketer in the team had been paid the same amount of money. Then contracts arrived and seniority and performance became factors in classifying players. Even then, your value was often in direct proportion to your current skill and differences in remuneration were actually an incentive to get better. In the IPL, because of the scarcity of certain kinds of players, and the need to play no more than four overseas players, there were huge variations in the kind of money that colleagues were earning. A player earning 10 crores could be batting alongside someone earning 10 lakhs. Worse still, a legend could be earning 2 crores and a far lesser Indian player could be earning three times the money. The possibility of fissures within the team was enormous and part of the leader's job was to maintain the right spirit within the team. One year, after Chennai Super Kings had won the IPL, M. S. Dhoni said he was happiest at the fact that even though many good players had to be on the bench, the team spirit was positive! Just another small illustration of the role of a leader during change!

Rather sadly, young, relatively untested players who got huge amounts in the auction because their skill was suddenly in scarcity, found themselves living under the burden of their incomes which, as it turns out, they hadn't asked for but had accidentally got. They believed they had to live up to their current valuation; everyone was talking about it, newspapers were measuring returns they were offering and to that extent they were like an over-priced stock. So, before they took the field, they were already a wreck, playing now to justify their cost rather than simply for the joy and excitement of taking wickets or scoring runs. The pressure was coming from elsewhere and quite a few players who were fortunate to land such life-changing contracts couldn't cope and fizzled out. It might be a stretch to make this comparison, but young managers who have to play for the returns that sustain their ballooning EMIs soon find that their choice of workplace was dictated by the wrong considerations!

It also took time to come to terms with the fact that players you had played against were now team-mates with whom you conferred on how to get out one of your erstwhile colleagues, and maybe a friend. Virender Sehwag and Shoaib Akhtar had a fairly well-known and colourful rivalry when they played against each other for India and Pakistan. But then, Shoaib came to play for the Kolkata Knight Riders (KKR) and his Indian team-mates could have been forgiven, at least initially, for having conflicting thoughts when he ran in to bowl to Sehwag of the Delhi Daredevils! Certainly, Yuvraj Singh was ruffled enough in the first season of the IPL when he was booed by the Mumbai crowd (when he played against the Mumbai Indians) to say 'I am an India player too'. But, he wasn't there in that role!

And so teams lost the borders they traditionally had and team-building became a rather more complex issue. Earlier, teams used to be fairly homogeneous and all of a sudden, there were Australians, South Africans, Trinidadians and Sri Lankans sharing a dressing room and travelling with players from Delhi, Bengaluru and Ranchi. Not only did they speak different languages, but had markedly different approaches to life. The Aussies thought nothing about having a couple of beers post the game, occasionally more, while the young Indians wondered some times and regretted at other times! Also, every team spent a lot of time getting its players to understand and respect each other and it led to interesting results.

Corporate India went through this phase when the workforce began attracting bright young people from areas they didn't normally source from. And as businesses went global, they needed to be sensitised to the culture they were working in.

As we saw in the previous chapter, one of the companies we worked with in the South, for example, had to begin trusting people who didn't speak Tamil! Because they had been so homogenous all along, everyone spoke the same language, had the same festivals and probably had the same ambitions for their children. Sometimes, such teams can become clannish, one within themselves but cut off from the outside world.

But, there is a positive to heterogeneous groups too and that is something that businesses in an increasingly smaller world will relate to. A heterogeneous team is often the most conducive environment for learning and as Ajinkya Rahane realized, there were things to be learnt beyond mere batting or fielding. 'The Australians know how to keep their emotions in check whether they they win or lose. Indians tend to feel the highs and lows a lot more', he observed.[2] In the IPL kind of format, with a match every day and no time to brood over a loss or get carried away by a win, this must be a useful skill to pick up. It was a wonderful opportunity for young Indian players to watch international legends from such close quarters.

The league also welcomed talented players like Shakib-al-hasan and Mustafizur Rahman, who coming from a smaller team like Bangladesh rarely got a chance on big stage. Yet, much like the rest of the VUCA (volatile, uncertain, complex and ambiguous) world, opportunity coexisted with vulnerability, with many players being picked for a single season, never to get picked again. Some other single season successes like Swapnil Asnodkar or Paul Valthaty discovered that if they didn't maintain success, the axe came just as quickly as the initial opportunity had.

Because teams were constructed from diverse skills and achievement levels, people could learn from each other and, just as important, become sensitive to each other's culture. The South African player Faf du Plessis said he wanted to learn from the Australian Michael Hussey and, in a sense, looked upon the IPL as a six-week on-the-job course. I am sure it was the same with Sachin Tendulkar at the Mumbai Indians and Jacques Kallis at Kolkata Knight Riders. Suresh Raina learnt from Mathew Hayden and Ajinkya Rahane was desperate to play for the Rajasthan Royals because he wanted to play with and learn from Rahul Dravid. And David Warner realised he could become a test player in the course of a conversation with Virender Sehwag! So maybe that was another reason for the allure of playing for Manchester United. The opportunity of having Alex Ferguson show you the way or chisel your game!

This was an example of senior players drawing talent towards themselves. It is possible too, in corporate life, that influential leaders and entrepreneurs become magnets for young talent; that young managers keep their beloved 'package' at bay and, in a manner of speaking, sit by the feet of the guru and learn. But, the gurus need to be givers too and need to make time for young managers. Increasingly, in the ridiculously long and extremely unhealthy working hours it insists on, corporate India is squeezing young talent rather than growing it. If all the time is used up in chasing jobs, how will innovation happen? How will the mavericks stun you with their out-of-the-box thinking?

In a sense, the IPL is like a multi-disciplinary, multi-country team project. You work together for a common objective for a couple of months, feed off each other, and go back to your normal job with a more homogenous composition.

While the format of T20 cricket, and in the IPL, the composition of teams, was vastly different from anything known before, the greatest innovation has come in the playing and in the measurement of cricket. As Suresh Raina said when he was playing for Chennai Super Kings, '*Yeh toh chaalis ball ka game hai*!' (This is a game of 40 balls!). It lead to a vastly different assessment of risk and, as a consequence, to the arrival of different shots, different balls bowled and the explosion of analytics. The last is the most interesting one. Cricket has always been a game that lent itself to measurement. But in T20, because every ball was an event, every over was 5 per cent of the innings, you needed to measure more accurately and use analytics in decision making. While instinct will never go out of a leader's repertoire, and mustn't, analytics is allowing him to be more precise than mere hypothesis could have.

The maximum innovations in the playing of T20 cricket have come in shot-making. It is interesting that each of these has come as a counter to traditional field placements and, except for the switch-hit which stretches the definition, none of them have broken the rules of the game. Each of these shots came from players who challenged existing thought and recalibrated risk. As you read of these, think of similar situations in corporate life where you are predictable and cumbersome because you follow the dictum of 'It's always been that way'. Think also of start-ups that have adopted fresh, unconventional approaches to business and are tied down by far fewer taboos than established businesses.

When we were young, we were always taught to play in the 'V'. (That of course was when we played on proper pitches otherwise crouching low and playing forward could lead to a broken nose!). That 'V' was between mid-off and mid-on or at best, between extra cover and mid-wicket. We were told that we must, at all times, endeavour to show 'the maker's name' to the bowler (meaning you play with such a straight bat that the bowler can read what is written on your bat). Hitting the ball in the air was also frowned upon because it was merely another way of getting out. We were actually told that hitting a six was like having a drink (remember this was an era where 'having a drink' meant you were loose and wild!) and that it would tempt you into another and ultimately lead you towards doom. 'The great Don Bradman hit only six sixes over his entire test career', we were often reminded.

You could understand the thinking, akin to never taking a loan, keeping money in secure fixed deposits and spending very carefully. It was essential in a less affluent India and that translated into playing safe, almost predictable cricket. But, once someone challenged the givens, we realised that some of the shots routinely frowned upon weren't actually as dangerous as previously assumed. And they were profitable. In the early days of the 'Dilscoop', Ian Chappell who was commentating on television joked, 'I hope he has a good dentist!'

The shot, over the wicket-keeper's head was, if well executed, a pretty safe one because there was never going to be a fielder there. So, in effect, batsmen were discovering newer markets and exploiting them. And soon, a new 'V' was being formed: behind the batsman! AB de Villiers emerged as the game's first genuine 360-degree batsman, a phrase impossible to even imagine a generation earlier.

It meant too that traditional field placement had to change because disruption in strokeplay could not be countered with a conventional approach. Bowlers started to feel the heat because the same ball could be hit over mid-wicket or reverse-swept to third man. And a relook at conventional risk meant that a 50-50 shot (meaning an equal chance of the shot coming off or the batsman getting out), hitherto frowned upon was now on. Batsmen were looking for more gaps, not just between fielders as they were taught to by the old masters but in the space between the fielder and the sky above. And batsmen discovered, as bowlers did to their sadness, that by confronting traditional thought, newer results were coming forth, that with the arrival of technology (in the form of big but not very heavy bats), you could recalibrate risk.

At the heart of this re-evaluation of risk, was the fact stated earlier—every ball is an event and every over is 5 per cent of the match. Not taking a risk was expensive too because a dotball was a setback. Also, since you had ten wickets to lose over a mere twenty overs, batsmen were more dispensable. Matches also followed each other with greater frequency and so the sadness at being out cheaply today was quickly dispelled by the opportunity of batting again in a couple of days.

It is noticeable too that it required a maverick like Dilshan, like Kevin Pietersen, Virender Sehwag or AB de Villiers to introduce change. Such mavericks exist everywhere but only find support for their thinking in some organisations. Sehwag says he was encouraged to bat the way he did because of all the greats following him in the order and often requests CEOs to let younger managers take a chance. 'In case anything goes wrong, you are there!' he says to applause from the young and a smile from the bosses! But, it does draw attention to the way mavericks are treated. If they are crushed, the message goes out to everyone that they must conform. Pietersen called his then coach a woodpecker. 'He was at me all day. Peck-peck, peck-peck, peck-peck … I had to tell him to leave me alone.'[3] Understanding people like Pietersen wasn't easy but he was a match-winner. Handling talents who look at the world differently is a big management challenge and sometimes people are unaware of the cost of ignoring it.

With every ball having an impact on the game, teams started measuring things more carefully and the role of analytics, so crucial in T20 cricket, is only going to grow.

Today, you can measure strike rates of a batsman to balls pitched in different areas at different speeds and can plan bowling to him accordingly. So too are captains changing batting orders to ensure that players are batting at a time when their strike rate is likely to be the highest. One season at the IPL, the Australian Brad Hodge suddenly moved from opening the batting to coming down at No. 6. When asked about it he said, 'I'm the Aussie in the team. I bat when the bowling is fast.'[4] His team had worked out that with spinners bowling early on, his low strike rate against spin would be a liability but that he could be a match winner in the last five overs when the quicker bowlers bowl.

In their topsy-turvy run at the IPL of 2016, it was noticeable that the Royal Challengers bowled Stuart Binny for only one over (only occasionally two), often the first of the innings. The analytics show that the first is the wait-and-see over and fewest runs are scored off it and so you can slip an over in from someone who might be expensive later on.

Players are also assessed differently now because analytics allow you to do that. For eg., if a bowler has figures of 4-0-32-0 and another has 4-0-41-0 the easy assessment is that the first has bowled better. But, analysts look at the average scoring patterns in the specific overs bowled. If bowler 1 has, say, bowled overs number 1,7,9,12 and the sum of the average run rates for these overs is, say, 28, he has actually gone over-par. On the other hand, if bowler 2 bowls overs 5, 16, 18 and 20 and the average runs/over for those is 45, he has done well and is maybe, more valuable than bowler 1!

Moneyball has arrived in T20 cricket where you no longer only gun for stars but for the bit player who is capable of game-changing performances. To be a match winner you need to have a great 20 minutes maybe. No more! The World T20 of 2016 was turned around by Carlos Brathwaite in four balls, the final of the IPL-2016 by Ben Cutting in a couple of overs. Sunrisers Hyderabad worked out that left-handers tended to be more effective and packed their side with them. At auctions, players are put into clusters (seam bowling all-rounders, >140 strike rate openers etc.) and bought accordingly because in a constructed team, you need some of each. Many teams do simulations of the auction process and algorithms aren't scoffed at.

Interestingly, with analytics, both teams have access to the same data and frequently, it is mined the same way too. (Number crunchers in companies will know that well!). So, after the tour of England in 2014, everyone realised that bowling a 4th or 5th stump line to Virat Kohli was the way to go because, among other things, his wagon wheel was full of leg-side shots. In 2016, that changed dramatically and Kohli, who must have seen identical data, worked on his game and became astonishingly good through the off-side. Wicket-taking balls became scoring balls!

With smaller boundaries, bigger bats and an open mind on possibilities, we have started seeing a virtual irreverence to targets. At IPL 2014, Mumbai Indians needed 190 in 14.5 overs to qualify and got there! We believe that among the many valid reasons for targets not being reached, the resistance in the mind is one. Corporate India is throwing up so many instances where audacious goals have been reached. Maybe that is the lesson from T20. Don't say no, because even the most difficult looking targets are being chased down!

The beauty of T20 and in particular, the IPL is that it has changed the look of cricket forever. The pace at which this format was being played has had a rub off on the test and one-day cricket as well. There are more 300+ scores than before in one-day internationals, 350 is being chased down and there are more results in test cricket. International cricket is more athletic than ever before. The IPL matches with their cheerleaders, their carnival like atmosphere, the celebrity-spotting courtesy the wealthy team-owners have upped the glamour quotient of the game. The IPL is as much about entertainment as it is about sport. Most of the matches end up with a close finish. Viewers find reasons to support multiple teams—it could be their local franchise, they could be fans of Chris Gayle or A. B. DeVilliers or even Shahrukh Khan or Preity Zinta! All this excitement has managed to ensure packed stadiums for most matches. Watching an IPL game is a family outing since women and youngsters are more open to watching this fast-paced version. T20 has given a new lease of life to cricket and is now the most profitable form of the game.

But perhaps the greatest connect with the corporate world is that in T20, and especially in the IPL, resources are being equalised. That is also what technology is doing to the modern world where connectivity and logistics are taking away traditional strengths and ensuring that teams that were underdogs by a traditional measure are now able to compete as equals. Where employees had to be laboriously trained for specific skills, buying from elsewhere (or in the auction like in the IPL) seems an easier option. It is disrupting many sectors and who knows, there might already be niche match-winners in offices!

The T20 revolution, and the growth of the IPL, was the outcome therefore of innovation that emerged from challenging the givens and keeping an open mind on all the possibilities that such a challenge could throw. Had cricket stayed wedded to its past and ignored the rapid changes in customer preferences, it might have been on the path towards becoming a marginal sport and would have been vulnerable to the choices being offered to a new generation. It is something managers need to keep abreast of, especially in this volatile and uncertain world.

Staying Relevant in a Changing World

- Status quo can be the solution but only if it is the outcome of rigorous examination.
- People hold on to what they know best because they are threatened.
- Challenging the givens is an integral part of innovation.
- When disruption is inevitable, you question yourself, your relevance and accept the need to adapt.
- During times of disruption, learning and unlearning both become critical
- A heterogeneous team is often the most conducive environment for learning
- It requires mavericks to introduce change. Such mavericks exist everywhere but only find support for their thinking in some organisations
- The hallmark of the VUCA world is that opportunity coexists with vulnerability
- While instinct will never go out of a leader's repertoire, and mustn't, analytics is allowing him to be more precise than mere hypothesis could have
- In the modern world, technology, connectivity and logistics are taking away traditional strengths and ensuring that teams that were underdogs by a traditional measure are now able to compete as equals.

Team Building

While the current thinking in business schools holds that all someone with an idea needs to succeed are focus, clarity and a good business plan, I have found that bringing together a great team that's united by strong motivation, determination and bravery is much more important.

—Richard Branson

One of the favourite past-times of sports-lovers is picking their dream teams. We've all done it and experienced the great power of holding someone's destiny in our hands! Picking a dream team is really about picking the best man for the position at that time, ideally an all-time great. The best thing about this exercise, apart from the fact that the 'team' is never going to take the field, is that nobody needs to give thought to issues like how a Garry Sobers could communicate with a Kapil Dev, for example, or whether Don Bradman would get along with Muttiah Muralitharan. Could Pele and Maradona have co-existed in the same team? How would Jayawardene have handled Shoaib Akhtar? Would Messi and Ronaldo have scored more goals if they had played together? All you know is that you have a team of your choice, or more precisely a collection of players, that you believe will be a winning collection.

In corporate life though, there is a major difference. Unless you are a start-up, most leaders inherit teams and these teams may not always be ideal. Most leaders wish their teams were like Manchester United or Barcelona playing together and generating quality performances day in and day out. Managers too aspire to work for top notch companies, say a Mahindra or a Google, because these organisations are seen as 'winning teams'. The truth is, while it's easy to spot a winning team or an employer of choice, building a champion side is unfortunately not as easy as picking your Dream Team.

The challenge is in knowing what makes these dream teams work, how we can make our team the Manchester United of retailing for example, or how to transform our bank into the Chelsea or Barcelona of finance, for these teams symbolise well-oiled, successful units.

The Building Blocks—Talent, Team Climate and Collective Pride

Very often, execution is the defining element and therefore the stumbling-block. It is one thing to know what to do, quite another to actually put that into practice. To be able to do that, you need good teams with good team-players, because quality execution often requires one set of people to help another set to deliver. The team must possess that work ethic and the players must be happy enough to follow it. So whether you are making a film, playing a competitive sport or running a company, the same three things go into making a good team; great talent, a healthy team climate that is conducive to performance, and collective pride. Contrary to what we have been made to believe in our growing-up years, talent by itself probably counts for the least because it can stagnate and rot when not nurtured properly but bloom and mature under the right conditions. Yes, talent is important but as we have seen earlier in the book, beyond a point it ceases to be a differentiator. Pride in the team, on the other hand, ensures that success is not one-time and the flock stays together happily to see many more wins.

Success is the magnet that attracts talent and resources. Performers want to work for companies that are on the list of best employers and companies want to be employers of choice. Venture capitalists are interested in fledgling companies that hold promise, clients want to associate themselves with big names, and suppliers in turn like to flaunt their top clients. It might seem like a chicken-and-egg situation but everyone wants winners or, as it seems, are in search of them!

The aura around winners is unmistakable, whether it's the swagger of a Viv Richards or a Virat Kohli, the cool confidence of a Roger Federer or M. S. Dhoni, the cockiness of Usain Bolt or Richard Branson or the understated charm of Sundar Pichai or Vishwanathan Anand. However, winners need to be in the right company as well. Thierry Henry didn't perform for France quite as well as he did for Arsenal. Messi was simply brilliant for Barcelona but not quite the same for Argentina. Directors make good films only with certain producers and interestingly, successful CEOs sometimes fail to recreate the magic when they move jobs.

It is interesting to try and see why that happens. The essence of good teams lies in the sense of belonging, in the ability to play for each other. Yet, people who possess all this find the urge to move jobs. Essentially people move because they are offered better terms somewhere else; they perceive a greater challenge, see greater power for themselves maybe, or they seek to fulfil an aspiration. There is nothing wrong with any of these things and people have made some very good moves for these reasons, but they need to be very sure that they will fit into a new set-up and into a fresh team ethic.

Glenn Maxwell confessed that when he moved to the relatively low profile Kings XI Punjab he found himself more comfortable and feeling wanted than when he was one among many performers in an already star-studded Mumbai Indians team. This sense of belonging is critical to a player's well-being and has to do more with the culture of the team rather than the performance of the player. It is really unfortunate that Kevin Pietersen despite being the top performer for England was always considered the outsider. It was as much a tragedy for England as it was for KP.

Coaches and corporate leaders are very often quoted as saying that they place attitude over talent. Talent is always easier to find since all our education is geared towards teaching us skills. Talent without the right attitude is like a stallion running amuck. Even though talent is over-rated, a team will struggle without it, while a player's attitude or the collective attitude of a team defines team spirit and determines where the team ends up. People who build good teams tend to use talent or ability as the first cut-off but thereafter strive strenuously to mould that ability into a strong team ethic. Alex Ferguson did that at Manchester United, M. S. Dhoni did it over a five-to-six-year period for India and captains and coaches have made that a benchmark for Australian cricket.

Surrendering the Me for the We

Attitude needs to be cultivated long-term and good teams are quick to encourage and reward good attitude while nipping errant behaviour in the bud. Pat Riley says that good teams become great when players trust each other enough to surrender the 'me' for the 'we'. It's an engaging thought. On the surface it doesn't seem like a long distance to cover but it can be a frightful distance for some teams. Often teams that seek to make a place for themselves in the sun start up as entrepreneurial ventures ; teams inching their way up the leagues display tremendous zeal and are united by the all-for- one-and-one-for-all approach. The biggest danger to the 'we' ironically comes with winning. The pursuit of success brings a team together but achieving it can sometimes be a poison pill and test a leader.

Success often breeds many owners. 'I took the two wickets that triggered the collapse', the bowler might say. The defence might claim that their steadfastness prevented a goal being scored, while the striker might point to the fact that eventually someone had to put the ball into the net. The hallmark of a good leader lies, therefore, not just in building a team but holding it together when the call for individual glory is sounded by some. That is why good leaders often point to trust as the most important ingredient in building a good team.

One of the biggest issues that HR managers in India are dealing with is that Indians don't make very good team-players. Mathew Hayden raised a storm when he said that Indian cricketers are selfish and play for personal milestones. 'But countries like India suffer from that. We back ourselves against those countries because they'll get two or three players in the 70s and beyond, and they'll be eyeing off that personal landmark and it'll cost their side 40 or 50 runs as a result ... In one-day cricket, the so-called landmarks like 50s and 100s are not achieved at the same rate as in Tests ... it's partnerships that can really hurt a side and set up a side.'

Hayden wasn't wrong, because there was a phase in

Indian cricket when the batsmen scored more centuries than anyone else but the team itself didn't have a record to match. By contrast, of the initial quartet of West Indies fast bowlers, Andy Roberts, Michael Holding, Joel Garner and Colin Croft, not one of them took 300 Test wickets, but collectively they were a lethal force. Michael Holding said to us that it didn't matter at the time who took a wicket as long as one of them did!

A popular explanation for this phenomenon is that our large population forces us to develop selfish instincts at every step. You cannot get into a bus or a train if you make way for someone else. The sheer amount of domestic cricket in India often forces selectors to look at individual scores rather than the situation of play. A gritty 32 when the team is in trouble may be more valuable than an 80 on a flat pitch against poor opposition, but inevitably the player who gets the 80 will catch the eye of the selector who hasn't been at the ground. In such a climate, a player who has become conditioned to put 'self' first is suddenly expected to subjugate his needs to those of the team when he plays at the national level. It cannot happen and therein maybe is the explanation for Hayden's observation.

One hypothesis is that in over-populated and therefore insecure countries, the self will always dominate. Feelings of comradeship, of surrendering the self to the wider cause, can only arise in either a highly spiritual phase or where the performer of great achievements has ascended to a level of personal calm about those achievements.

When you are in a mob, and all of us are in a mob sometimes, self-preservation will always prevail. When a team is performing, and therefore settled, and where individuals are secure, they can rise above the self and play for the cause. Indeed, playing for the cause then becomes a greater virtue.

Indians have to constantly compete for limited seats in both education and jobs. Marten Pieters, then MD and CEO of Vodafone, likes to think of Indians as individualistic rather than selfish. 'People are individualistic in all cultures. But in India you learn very young that you can only succeed more or less at the cost of someone else. Here you are happy to scream from the towers, "I am the best of the class". If you did that in Holland, people would hate you. It is more appreciated to be in line with the team than excel.'[1]

One of the clues to how good a team-player you are lies in how much you are willing to do for no reward, how hard you are willing to run as a non-striker or how much you are willing to push yourself to cut off a boundary or save a run. These are things that contribute to the performance of the team or your team mate, but not to your personal performance statistics. We asked Sachin how, as a captain and senior player, he evaluated players. It came as no surprise that the ultimate team-player said without any hesitation that he rates players by their commitment, rather than their performance. He says that effort is the only thing entirely in your control and that he has no respect for those unwilling to put that in.

Jerry Rao thinks that the punishment for flouting team rules in our part of the world is very low. Witness politicians being readmitted after being expelled, or players seemingly left out on disciplinary grounds being picked for big games. Clear communication of team rules and a low tolerance for deviation from these rules are critical to good team culture.

In their best years as a team, Pakistan were led by Imran Khan, who demanded a very high standard of team ethic. The story goes that in one of their always highly charged games against India at Sharjah, a batsman was sent out with clear instructions to go for it in the last two overs. Not having done too well in the earlier games the player was probably a bit insecure and opted to return not out rather than go with the riskier alternative of attacking and, maybe, getting out. As the players returned to the pavilion for lunch, Imran came down the steps towards the boundary rope and told the batsman loudly enough for everyone to hear, 'You will never play for Pakistan again.' The message was sent out as much to the player as to the rest of the team and indeed, to the opposition who were in earshot! This is a rare occurrence on the sub-continent and hence worthy of retelling.

'Surrendering the Me for the We' does not in any way imply that individuals must kill their own ambition. Far from it. It only suggests an alignment of individual goals with team goals and if there is a situation where these goals are in conflict, team goals must take precedence. It also suggests a culture of co-operation and helping those who are falling behind in performance (and there will always be such people or businesses) to improve and do better. During one of our corporate events, the managing director of a large FMCG company told us about a young executive in the firm who was promising but lacked certain skills that would allow him to fulfil his potential. The senior executives worked on him, there was lots of encouragement and some harsh words, but eventually he turned the corner and rose to an impressive position in the organisation and as the managing director of a company thereafter. In a 'me' kind of set-up no one would have bothered.

Some years ago when ESPN Star Sports (as it was then called) ran a programme called 'The Dream Job' (or 'Harsha ki Khoj'), we sat together to pick the winner. It was clear who the most talented was but when his name came up, the Head of Production vetoed it immediately. 'He'll never fit in a team, mate, and television is all about team work,' he said. As it turned out, the best candidate didn't win because there was too much 'me' in him.

Team Ethics

In the course of our programmes which, at the time of writing, are nudging 500, in number, we've had a sneak peek at most sectors including FMCGs, banks and other financial institutions, pharma, IT, consultancy, BPOs, entertainment, white goods and many others. In our opinion, the most challenging in terms of team-building was investment banking. The extreme competitiveness and high degree of confidentiality means that there is almost no trust or sharing within the team. The one thing that probably holds them together is that they all have the same company name on their visiting cards! In one such organisation we did a case study relating to teams. When the discussion started to go contrary to team-building principles, an impromptu question was thrown to the group and a secret vote taken. They were asked if they would commit a foul in the last minute of a football game if they were guaranteed a win, diving in the penalty area to fool the referee, for example. Close to half the group said that they would, the outcome clearly more important than the means! Sadly, sport seems to throw up as many situations where taking liberties with the law seems acceptable, as it does to others in other fields, where outstanding and ethical team values are ostensibly celebrated.

In another group, a pharma company this time, we were doing a case study on leadership. The situation was a difficult one in which the leader's neck was on the block. The star in the group refused to follow team rules but sacking him would mean that sales would take a big hit. On the other hand, keeping him would set the wrong precedent for the rest. The various groups came up with their solutions, debating what they should do. They didn't want the star but they needed him. The debate heated up and at one point one of the groups suggested that the leader lie to the rest of the group. Suddenly, many others seemed to agree till one gentleman, got up and said how appalled he was at such a suggestion. This led to a very interesting debate on team ethics which finally ended with the MD, who was merely a spectator till then, sternly making a point that he would never tolerate anything like this.

Nasser Hussain says his county side in Essex, England, faced a similar, if less distressing situation. Their top player refused to buy into the team ethic and as the matter dragged on, it began affecting the side. The issue was, do we say goodbye to 1500 runs a year and become a weaker side or put team values first? Eventually, Hussain says, the team had no choice but to say goodbye to the star since retaining him would have meant acceptance of this deviation from acceptable standards.[2]

England's team management, at the time, thought that was the issue with Kevin Pietersen, that he wasn't buying into the team ethic. In the chapter on leadership, you will see how sometimes by taking the trouble to understand people, the issue of self vs. the team can be resolved to the benefit of everybody.

It is a bit worrisome though, that increasingly in India we seem to accept expressions like *chalta hai* (anything goes) or *jugaad*—a word instantly recognisable to most Indians but without a suitable English equivalent—where getting things done seems to matter more than how those things are done.

Interdependence

In all businesses as in sport, there are always jobs or roles that are more visible and glamorous. Sales and marketing are like strikers who score goals and create records. Investment consultants are stars, like opening batsmen. HR and admin, like production and distribution, hardly make it to the front-page. In good companies, there is appreciation for the backroom boys who set it all up for the frontline people to achieve their targets. Without top performance from them, the chain would be weak and would affect the team's overall performance adversely.

Such then, is the importance of the holding mid-fielder in football. This player is the tireless runner whose job is to nip the opposition moves in the bud. Without getting onto the score sheet, without making the dramatic goal-line save, the mid-fielder stands like a rock and is only really noticed when absent.! Just as it is with a good HR manager, the mid-fielder is an integral part of all good teams and among the earliest to be on the team sheet. To that extent this player is like a good non-striker who is the key to rotating the strike in a partnership, and ensures that the better player has more of the strike.

In fact, the role of the non-striker was best brought out by Glenn McGrath when he said that five out of Steve Waugh's 32 centuries should actually be his because if he had not hung around at the non-striker's end, there was no way Waugh could have scored them! A star can perform only if he is properly supported by the team and that is why setting up a goal is as important as scoring one. If each one tries to score by himself, the team will cease to even function as a team, let alone do well.

So if Virat Kohli is at the non-striker's end while Chris Gayle is blasting the opposition at the other end, as happened often with the Royal Challengers Bangalore, it would be best if he gave the strike to Gayle at the earliest opportunity rather than getting into a competition to show he is as good a batsman as Gayle—which no doubt he is—and acknowledged that that particular day clearly belonged to Gayle. (It need hardly be emphasised that this attitude would work if when Kohli was blasting away, Gayle offered him the strike!)

Mukul Deoras says that one of the tools HUL strongly believed in (from his experience in working there before becoming head of Colgate Palmolive) is listening to the people on the ground and helping them with the right resources. Formerly an avid cricketer himself, he adds, 'Even the best bowler needs the best field placement'.[2]

The fact is that the fielders inside the circle often create the wicket! By cutting off the singles, they force the batsman to play a more dangerous shot and in doing so are effectively setting it up for the bowler to eventually get the wicket. In every good team one arm sets it up for the other to finish. The mid-fielders lay the ball for the striker to score, the batsmen put the runs on the board for the bowlers to bowl freely, and the bowlers keep the runs down so the batsmen have a smaller target to chase. A keeper standing up might force a batsman to play from the crease, which is what the bowler wants!

Michael Jordan often went away from the ball and created openings for the others to score.

With the growing importance of fitness in sport, even the physios and masseurs are in a sense setting up the goal for the players to score, putting them back in action in the minimum possible time. It is important for leaders to be aware though that players will happily set up a goal for someone else to score if the team climate, created by the leader of course, is such that those that set it up are rewarded too. If you only reward the player who scores, nobody will pass.

In the FIFA World Cup of 2006, France tended to play with a lone striker in Thierry Henry. In their quarter-final, the skillful and younger Spaniards planned to play the off-side trap against him to try and negate him. Aware of this, Henry kept playing closer and closer to the half-line and in doing so, kept drawing the defence further up field. When the moment came, Patrick Viera slipped a ball through to the young and lightning-fast Franck Ribery who went through virtually unchallenged through the off-side trap. On the face of it, Ribery scored the goal after a lovely pass from Viera, but it was set up by Henry who was happy to play off the ball and create an opening for someone else.

Holding Teams Together

In creating the 'we', integrating all the diverse groups is critical. Diversity enriches teams by bringing in varied cultures and ways of approaching issues. We see that in the IPL where a Trinidadian sits in the same dressing room as a Sri Lankan and, wonder of wonders, Australians and New Zealanders discuss strategy together. Along with them is the Test star from Bengaluru, but also a young kid from Jharkhand and an inexperienced young man from Vijayawada who might be in awe of the bigger stars. The job of the leader is therefore to ensure that there is free mingling of players to enhance knowledge and also to build team spirit. If the stars are aloof, or worse, disrespectful, it can create discord and dissent within a side. In diverse teams like in the IPL, or in many global projects, the role of the leader becomes even more critical.

If there are people who have doubts about whether diversity is really good for the team or not, they need to look at the IPL where all players have benefitted from this 'cross-pollination'. Top international cricketers get to showcase their talent in a tournament that is, sometimes, more competitive and high pressure than international cricket while impressionable young Indian players get to play alongside and learn from the best in the world.

It seems to be true as well that maximum learning occurs in diverse teams because not only do people come with different skills, they carry different approaches to doing things. Once exposed to them, players can decide whether that works for them but at least they will have realised that there is another way of doing things. An Indian player told us in 2016, for example, that every

IPL team must have 'a West Indian because they just play differently!'

While diversity can be enforced, inclusion needs to work in spirit. People tend to be comfortable with those who are like them. They avoid people who think differently or are from different backgrounds and ask uncomfortable questions. That is human behaviour but when leaders only recruit managers who are replicas of themselves, there is a problem. 'That's what I call a coterie, not a team,' says V. R. Ferose of SAP Labs.[3] First came the realization that women, who are now a sizeable proportion of the workforce, needed to be treated equally, yet differently. Now managers in their 40s and 50s are finding that Gen Y employees have different motivations and different concepts about loyalty and work-life balance. People from smaller towns are now making it to the better institutes and the bigger companies. They have the qualifications and the hunger but not quite the grooming or the urban accent. Mavericks are great for innovation but don't like office rules. Global teams now consist of people who are diverse in nationality, religion, gender, generation, culture, skills and temperament. They need to be embraced and integrated into the team. It would be sad to see more talent go the Kevin Pietersen way.

In sport, certainly in cricket, the tradition was to get players from different backgrounds to share rooms. This prevented groupism and helped players get exposure beyond their own city or region. Joy Bhattacharjya tells an endearing story from his days with the Kolkata Knight Riders. In 2012 he, along with coach Dav Whatmore, devised an ice-breaker activity where on a bus ride each player had to share something about his life that nobody knew about. Some players spoke in English, others in Hindi. There were laughs and tears and lots that got shared. To their surprise this also resulted in some unexpected bonding between the most unlikely people—Chris Lynn, a batsman from Queensland and Iqbal Abdulla, a spin bowler born in Azamgarh, both players discovering that they had similar backgrounds, having grown up as simple village boys. Paddy Upton too talks about how as coach of Rajasthan Royals he made every effort to get the voice of the youngest players heard. Not only did Paddy listen to their views but also shared them with the rest of the team during team meetings. The seriousness with which they were heard and the importance they were given gave the youngsters the confidence to speak up, sometimes despite obvious communication challenges.

CEOs too have now begun to acknowledge that frontline managers are in the best position to catch trends and competitive activity. But they need to be given a voice and a hearing by the seniors. If the culture in the organization doesn't encourage juniors to speak up or allow any debate, they will either keep their views to themselves or try and second-guess what the bosses would like to hear. A band of caring dissenters will be a more formidable team than an army of uncaring followers.

A climate of camaraderie reduces perceived risk in situations when teams are trying something new or innovative. All experiments come with risk attached and the feeling that we are all in it together only helps share the risk. The Sri Lankans demonstrated that at the 1996 cricket World Cup. More recently, Germany showed in the 2006 and 2010 World Cups that if everyone buys into a plan, the results can be thrilling. If either side had players who were not inclined to buy in they would not have played with the same freedom. And Leicester City's scarcely believable run to the Premiership in England in 2015-16 is a case study of what is possible when players within teams play for each other.

Marten Pieters, who spent a fair bit of time in India, remembers his early days here and the changes he needed to introduce. 'Earlier decisions were taken on a one-to-one basis (with one's boss). Now it's more team management. Initially, when people said they liked this new way of team management, I said that it wasn't so simple. It's far easier to convince one person (your boss) rather than all your colleagues. Team management is an effort. It sounds a bit slow but once you have decided on it, implementation is far easier. Everybody buys into the decision and then you move very quickly. You spend more time in the beginning but far less in the execution. The earlier system had quicker decisions but needed a lot more fixing in between because it wasn't well thought through.'[4]

While consensus is always desirable, it's often not

achievable. Those who disagree can sometimes wait for the project to fail just to prove themselves right. Leaders should listen to all the viewpoints and then take a call. Once the decision has been taken, there needs to be alignment for the project to succeed. If coalition governments can function like that, why not teams? Consensus may not be 100 per cent but commitment has to be. It is a great line and at the heart of team spirit. You may disagree with a leader's decision but once it is taken, and binding on the team, you give your best to make it possible.

Jerry Rao says you can see the 'band of boys' culture in winning teams. Subroto Bagchi calls it 'tribal identity'—common enemy, common and unique language, even common jokes! They have a shared vision and build this tribal identity for themselves. The West Indies cricketers of the late seventies and eighties (from an era where the national team was the only team you played for) drew strength from their identity as black cricketers. They talked about making their people proud by their performances. Viv Richards even spoke of knowing his history and of colonisation. Such strong feelings can only exist amidst homogeneity and modern day teams would need to look at other ways of bonding.

So too with Pakistan who displayed a rare sense of togetherness when playing against India and this enabled them to play fearlessly in matches where fear could well have been the defining emotion. Co-operation and togetherness, irrespective of the binding theme, makes the team more than the sum of its parts. This is when it becomes possible to achieve stretch goals by extracting maximum value out of the group.

The key to trust and co-operation within a team is fairness and equality. Steve Waugh says that when he was captain, he treated players 'equally but differently'. Since each person in the team is different and comes with his/her strengths and weaknesses as well as his/her own likes and dislikes, the leader needs to personalise his approach to suit the person. Yet, when it comes to team ethics, discipline, training and the like, the rules are the same, irrespective of whether you are the star player or the senior most team member. Those rules are the non-negotiables.

It is an interesting approach. Thus, while it was mandatory for a McGrath or a Warne to be part of the same training sessions as everyone else, they probably got the end they wanted to bowl from or the field they specifically wanted; little things that make the stars, the match-winners, feel important. However, by insisting that they were on time for, say, the team bus, (even the captain Steve Waugh was left behind one day!) they ensured that there was no resentment among the others. It is amazing how much discord little things like unpunctuality can lead to, in a team situation.

Conflict is natural in any group of people and teams would be lying if they claimed that they have never faced any. Sports teams tend to spend a lot of time together and given the adrenalin on which they thrive, are bound to get into arguments. The Australian cricket team at its peak had a lot of strong personalities, not all of whom got along. Shane Warne says it's all right if you are not best friends with your teammates as long as you respect them and what they bring to the team and don't carry your differences onto the field.

Stars Can Make or Break a Team

People like Sachin Tendulkar, Rahul Dravid and Anil Kumble, often acknowledged as some of the greatest players the game has seen, are also wonderful examples of players with impeccable team ethic. Tendulkar often tells the younger players he might be batting or training with, to point out any mistakes he might be making. 'They might hesitate to tell me,' he says 'so it is best I tell them upfront; much better to tell me before I am out rather than after!'

Players with a bad attitude, however talented they may be, can prove to be a burden on the team. While the team needs them as match-winners, they could end up harming the team in the long run by spoiling team dynamics. Shoaib Akhtar, some said, was one such player, capable of winning matches for his team with his searing pace but equally capable of affecting team climate by his behaviour.

When the Republic of Ireland qualified for the FIFA World Cup in 2002, their only major star was Manchester United's Roy Keane, a fiery, temperamental character.

He complained during training and eventually stormed out of the squad. Far from being demoralised by this, the team actually came together! The manager, Mick McCarthy, wrote, 'It has taken Keane eight full days to finally do what he tried to do in Saipan last Tuesday night and quit the World Cup, international football and the green jersey. He has tortured and tormented so many of us in the days and nights since then, perhaps even himself. He has walked away from the players he captained ...' He went on to say, 'The players are furious that the FAI (Football Association of Ireland) would even consider a return for Roy Keane after everything he said and did. Several of them are adamant that they will go home if Keane is imposed on us ... the players won't have him back. They are happy without him.'[5]

As Neeraj Garg says, 'If some people in the team believe that they bring more to the table than others, it results in a fractured team.' Even if people come from different areas, the value that they bring to the team must be on par. The roles they play may be different; some might seem to have more critical roles than others, but every role must be respected. Mutual respect makes collaboration easy and the camaraderie in the team is largely due to this respect that team members have for each other. Some players might think they only play small roles and are therefore not important enough. But without them, the team can lose a larger battle. You only have to see the pit-stop crew at a Formula One race to be convinced of this. A delay in changing tires could be the difference between winning and losing a race!

It is easy for the hugely talented and charismatic players to lapse into behaving like stars. In every team there are those who are more in the limelight than others, not only because of their role but also their personality. A star has the power to make or break a team. If he decides to act like a prima donna, throw his weight around and demand privileges outside of the team's rule book, it is natural that after a while the others will resent him. It's a strange situation then, when the team needs the star but his team mates don't want him, as with Keane. Most good teams, with good team-players, rally around the most valuable players so that the rest of the team can draw from their confidence and their knowledge. The Chicago Bulls eventually got there with Michael Jordan, as did the Los Angeles Lakers in the latter part of this decade with Kobe Bryant. The combination of the 'star' and the 'team' can sometimes seem like a tightrope act and that is why Nitin Paranjape is open in his praise of the Australian cricket team which he believes 'successfully marries individual brilliance with organisational consistency'.

Sometimes the star is hardly at fault but his aura is such that other players just naturally keep their distance or show their reverence. Hockey coach Oltmans tells a hilarious story of a player who most obviously passed to the wrong player. 'He is a senior player and he asked for the ball, so I passed,' the player innocently justified.

We saw a good example of the cult of the individual and the desire to reward the star, at the felicitation ceremony of the Indian team after winning the inaugural ICC World T20. While each player got a handsome purse, Yuvraj Singh was given a huge additional sum and an expensive car for hitting six sixes in an over. Admittedly, it was an outstanding performance, but there were other players who had played match-winning roles and they could easily have raised the banner of protest. At a time when the team was being celebrated, the cult of the individual was being thrust upon everyone.

Many years prior to this, after India had lost a Test match early on the fifth day in Melbourne, the hugely respected former Australian captain and later television broadcaster Mark Taylor, was walking back to the team hotel when he saw a group of Indian fans celebrating there. When asked what it was they were celebrating, he was told that it was in honour of a Tendulkar century ('best batsman in the world, mate ...' they went). It didn't seem to matter who had won the match as long as Tendulkar had done well.

It was a powerful example of how we can sometimes glorify the individual ahead of the team. No surprise then that when fans recall Sachin's 100th hundred at Mirpur, they don't remember that India lost that one-dayer to Bangladesh!

Continuous Improvement

Another indicator of good team climate is the desire to improve continuously—both as individuals and as a team in all aspects of the business. In the world of cricket, there is tremendous appreciation for teams like Sri Lanka and South Africa that came on to the international scene later than the others (especially for South Africa post their return to international cricket) but took very little time to catch up. Teams like Kenya and Bangladesh on the other hand had enough opportunities but lagged behind everyone else and indeed, it took Bangladesh many years to start making the move up.

Teams like Australia, which were on top for a long time, work very hard to stay two steps ahead at all times. The desire to excel can only materialize if the team is willing to stretch and is open to trying out new things. Coaches and captains keep healthy competition alive by keeping the team on its toes. Competition stays healthy when members try to excel by doing the best they can and not with a view to outdo each other at any cost. Good teams make it clear to their members that their real competition is their counterparts from competing teams, not their own team mates. So an opening batsman competes not with the other opener in his team but with openers from the competing team. At one level it may not be bad to spur competition among individual players but it can very quickly lead to a situation where trying to outdo each other becomes paramount, even at the cost of what the team really needs.

While leadership and decision-making determines how agile the team is, it's the young blood in the organization that makes it contemporary and with the times. This is truer in today's world of rapidly changing technology and innovation in every aspect of the business. Middle and senior managers who are out of sync with the new world are proving to be stumbling blocks in the team's improvement. We know of several cases where bright youngsters have quit top organisations since their ideas were being muzzled by their dinosaur bosses. Not because the ideas were not up to the mark but because the bosses didn't want to admit that they were beyond their comprehension!

The VUCA world, as experts like to label it is uncertain, changing and largely technology-driven and so our tomorrow is likely to look very different from today. As a result there is much crystal-ball gazing about how the workplace of the future will look. Will the idea of loyalty change with people being simultaneously part of multiple teams? Will employees identify with a function rather than an organization? Would CEOs be significantly younger? Would lots of jobs and businesses get obsolete—and with them people and skills as well? One thing is certain—adaptability and staying relevant would be the key to success. Adapt or perish could be a reality, not merely a cliché. T20 cricket did that to so many talented players since it required a different skillset from test cricket. Disruption is already happening in many businesses and the Goliaths of industry are fearful of the Davids lurking around the corner. Businesses are looking vulnerable and no one is too big to fail. Resilience then becomes a useful quality to possess. We have already discussed the side-effects of being successful. Adaptability is a challenge for those who have seen success and so is the ability to swallow failure.

With the democratisation of knowledge and ideas, the value of an employee would be based on his skills rather than his experience. Already, in T20 cricket, someone who can change a game in 20 balls is more important than someone who has been around for a while but can't produce an explosive innings. This could drastically change organizational as well as salary structures. Already in some companies, the CEO is not the highest paying employee. Sport is the ultimate meritocracy and anyone with skill can make it to the top, regardless of his age or background. 'My dream was to make Infosys a meritocracy like a cricket team,' Narayana Murthy confided in us.[6]

In the coming years Gen Y will outnumber Gen X and that will be another challenge to teams. Unlike Gen X, Gen Y looks for width of experience. They are more like all-rounders. Their motivations are different and they seek instant gratification. The principles of team culture, work ethic and engagement of employees will remain the same but the methodology is likely to be very different.

At the 2007 World Cup in the West Indies, Adam Gilchrist was having a patchy tournament in the run-up to the final. He says that at the team meeting before the big day he put his hand up and admitted he hadn't done too well. He was delighted when the team turned around and told him it didn't matter how much he or his partner Hayden scored individually, as long as they kept giving the team good starts. It was not about Gilchrist or Hayden but about the partnership. It put him in the right frame of mind to demolish the Sri Lankans in the final with an unforgettable innings.

Often we judge a good team as much by who is in it as by who isn't. It adds up. If the quality of people who cannot make the side is excellent, those in it must be even better. So the quality of the bench is a very good indicator of the quality of the side. A strong bench competing on performance alone can only add to healthy competition.

While a team with a strong bench is undoubtedly in an enviable position, it must also face up to the challenge of keeping the bench motivated. Talent sitting idle gets bored and, if not properly counselled, even disgruntled and disruptive. The initial years of the IPL saw franchises happily grab whatever talent they could lay their hands on. Of late, IPL franchises have resorted to keeping their squads lean. This way, they don't have to manage the large bench size and it helps keep the cost down as well. Maybe there's something there that IT companies could learn from.

The Australians often said that, at their peak, their second eleven was among the top three teams in the world. They like to stick it to the others, the Aussies, and were probably exaggerating, but if you expanded that statement to include the top five teams, the second eleven would comfortably have made it! When the West Indies were on top of the world, part of their aura came from some outstanding fast bowlers who were plying their trade in English county cricket, scaring the daylights out of many teams but with no chance of making their country's first eleven. In such a situation, aware that there are excellent replacements available, those fast bowlers that were in the team could have become insecure. A sure sign of such insecurity is if when you have done well, you don't want a team mate to do too well so that if someone has to be dropped it will be him, not you. When envy starts invading respect, the team is in trouble ... and yet there was great bonhomie among the four quicks and you can see that even today when they speak about each other. Roberts, Holding, Marshall and Garner were quite happy to help each other out and point out faults that might have crept up in the run up or in the delivery because, as Holding said, 'We were always aware of the fact that we were playing for the West Indies, that people all around the world were looking towards us to do well, and that was always there at the back of our minds'. In essence, it didn't matter who took a wicket as long as the team won. It is a wonderful, almost unparalleled team story.

Team Bonding

The ultimate test that the team is in good shape is the positive body language that creates the buzz in the dressing room. An optimistic attitude can be highly contagious. It manifests itself as the focus on the goal, the eagerness to deliver, seizing the opportunity and in going for the kill when the opposition is down. Winning teams are also thorough, adds Mukul Deoras, and no one leaves the small details for the other guy to sweat over. The 'can do' attitude is all pervasive and mates back each other, helping slow performers, co-mentoring and valuing each other's opinions. This, according to Sandip Das, is the sign that such teams are secure and apolitical. Trusting, caring and sharing are not merely buzzwords but on display for all to experience. Sometimes we wish these were taught in top management schools as well!

Communication is the final barometer to test team health. Lack of communication, or one-way communication, can spell trouble for any team. Ideally, communication would involve clarity of goals and roles, a respect for the views of all team members, a climate conducive to debate and discussion and finally, walking the talk. The last is critical. 'I think there is too much pampering in English cricket, too much of a focus on saying the right things when doing the right things is far more important,' Nasser Hussain said about the England cricket team when he was captain.[7] Nasser believes that it's always better that things are said and no one's left in any doubt. In an interview with Graham Hayday in 2001, he said that this kind of behaviour led to a 'matey' dressing room but he didn't think it would help them get any better.

This 'mateyness' in the dressing room, though not

sufficient, is a necessary condition for performance. Winning teams have to be happy teams. This means that team mates enjoy each other's company and like to spend time with each other even beyond working hours. Success stories and a common goal bind them together and go into making the third requirement for winning teams, collective pride.

Many corporate teams now tend to be huge and global, and meetings are virtual. Technology has made staying in touch really easy and cheap but is that a good substitute for mateyness? Marissa Mayer restarted the debate on remote work and whether social connections are important to team bonding. Virtual meetings do the job but are clearly structured and strictly scheduled and many argue that some of the best ideas come around the water cooler and strong bonds are built on the team bus or at the bar! Global teams though have no option and the communication challenge has to be met through the effective use of technology—'humanizing' technology , as Sandip Das calls it.

One of the signs of happy and successful team-bonding is the pride that individuals have in not only their own success but also in that of their team mates. There is no greater joy for a batsman than to look up at a balcony full of team mates cheering for him on his century. John Wright, former New Zealand captain, insisted that individual success be celebrated collectively when he became coach of the Indian cricket team. Sceptics may see this as forced behaviour, but in the long run it breaks down barriers and inhibitions and becomes second nature. We're all like that. We like people applauding us and when they do so, our resistance to applauding them diminishes!

Collective Pride

Collective pride over the team's success is the best glue any team can wish for. Performing the Hakka, wearing the baggy green or sporting the India jersey are privileges that are priceless. Reliving a successful team climate and recounting the experiences and challenges of winning, reinforces the team bond apart from generating confidence. People work not merely for salaries and perks, but for good companies, as more and more organisations are discovering!

Building employee engagement is central to an organisation's success. As the scale of business increases, junior employees struggle to see how their work contributes to the overall goal or strategy. There is a disconnect, as they are unable to connect the dots and see the big picture. Creating a higher purpose, contributing to the greater good is much more motivating for people as compared to merely having a job. Playing for India in the Davis Cup always made Leander Paes raise his game a few notches higher, he said. Virat Kohli went out of the way to label his fast bowlers the 'real heroes' because he knew that they could start believing that it was only the spinners who won matches while playing at home.

A good football club has a following that is loyal through its wins and losses. Loyalty that goes beyond remuneration is what insures companies against poaching from competitors and the key to this insurance is collective pride since not all team wins make all members happy. 'The Disease of Me' is known to make frequent visits even to good teams.

Finally, as Rahul Dravid says, the team is like a pot. Some people put into the pot, others draw from it. Who puts in and who takes out depends on the people as well as the moment. Ultimately, a team that has more people putting in rather than taking out is a happy team, a team more likely to win.

Who Is a Team Player?

One who:

- has a 'greater-than-me' perspective;
- puts more into the team pot than he takes out;
- is willing to give up the 'me' for the 'we';
- is willing to pass the ball especially when the other guy is in a better position to score;
- is willing to play in whatever position the team requires him to;
- gives 100 per cent, every time, under all circumstances;
- plays by the team rules;
- is encouraging and is happy to see team mates do well;
- is proud of belonging to his team;

Leadership

Inventories can be managed, but people must be led.

—H. Ross Perot

Wasim Akram, Pakistan's most successful fast bowler, with 414 Test wickets and 502 one-day wickets, retired from international cricket in 2003. But even today, when he receives a call from the legendary Imran Khan, Pakistan's most successful cricket captain, Wasim straightens up and replies with a reverential 'Skipper!' Pakistan, in spite of its immense cricketing talent, won practically nothing of significance before Imran Khan's captaincy and had to wait seventeen years after he retired to win the T20 World Championship in 2009. There must have been a reason, because they have never been short of ability. That is why the making of successful leaders, in sports as in business, is something that has always been hotly discussed and debated.

Some people make natural leaders. Others simply fail to inspire. Maybe they believe that those who play international sport should be good enough to understand what to do; or maybe they think that if a player needs to be inspired he is the wrong person to have in the team anyway; or maybe they just cannot understand people! Oddly, we've noticed that the most successful players, more often than not, were not very effective captains— while a successful captain like Mike Brearley or a coach like John Buchanan hardly seemed the most qualified for the job. Yet their scholarly ways, quite in contrast with Imran's charisma, seemed to have made a difference.

Often leadership is perplexing. Winston Churchill, who is remembered as one of the finest leaders during World War II, lost the elections that immediately followed the end of the war. One who made a great wartime leader was rejected as a peacetime manager! Adolf Hitler led, so did the gentle Nelson Mandela.

Reflecting changes in society, cricket, which earlier drew captains from more privileged backgrounds, made way for more middle-class captains. For a long time, England made a distinction between 'Gentlemen' and 'Players'. The former were aristocracy or gentry. There was a time when that's where you needed to have come from to become captain of the English cricket team and it wasn't till 1952 that a professional or a 'Player', Len Hutton, was appointed the captain. If you needed to earn money from the sport, it was felt, you were probably of the wrong stock! India, taking its cue from England, had princes as captain on its tours to England before Independence, ahead of cricketers who were more qualified but seemingly, of lower birth.

Even Mansur Ali Khan Pataudi, as it turns out, one of India's greatest captains, got the job at 21 because he was seen to have the right background. In later years, Mohammed Azharuddin and Mahendra Singh Dhoni became captains without anyone raising an eyebrow despite their relatively modest backgrounds.

The Role of the Leader

In the course of our sessions, we have often debated whether leadership is something people are born with or indeed, if it can be learnt; whether it is a natural or an acquired skill. We believe that there are certain aspects that come along with your DNA or your background. Traditionally in Asia, with its more feudal societies, people needed to look up to a leader as they did in the days gone by to the local chieftain or the prince. In families, fathers were looked up to and were never really one of the boys at home! Over the years, bosses started being called by their first names and now with CEOs getting younger and workplaces becoming less formal, leaders too look less distant. The era where the leader needed to belong to a certain social class has thankfully gone ; certainly it has in Indian cricket since M. S. Dhoni and in India in general after Narendra Modi!

However, there are other aspects to leadership (and these are quite a few) that can be understood, acquired and practised. Understanding the role of the captain is also important and while different situations require leaders to display various leadership qualities in different measures, there are certain things that form the core.

I suppose leadership at one time meant muscles; but today it means getting along with people.

—Mahatma Gandhi

A leader's skill lies in understanding players, in bringing out the best from each player, and in doing so, seeing that the whole adds up to more than the sum of the parts. Michael Holding told us that the reason Clive Lloyd was so respected was that he took the trouble to understand each player and to respect the fact that each person was different. It wasn't a one-size-fits-all style. It was said that Mike Brearley, on the basis of his ability alone, might not have made it to the English team but while being captain, he ensured that his star player Ian Botham was, effectively, worth two players.

We asked Virender Sehwag, who couldn't have been too easy to understand given the maverick he was (and actually is!), how he handled players when he was captain. 'You have to understand them,' he said. 'For example, if Gautam Gambhir hadn't scored runs in a few games, I would try and hurt him so that he went out to bat intent on proving me wrong. But with Dinesh Karthik (who played under him in IPL 1), I explained things, we talked about his strengths and weaknesses because that works for him.'[1] These were people driven by different emotions and so as captain you can't have a one size fits all approach to everyone. Again, like with Lloyd, Sehwag had probably taken the trouble to understand the person behind each player.

Gen X managers leading teams that consist largely of Gen Yers would agree that not only is the generation cut from a different cloth but their motivations too are different. Gen Xers—managers in their 40s and 50s are what are commonly referred to as the 'bees' generation. They largely stuck to similar job profiles and sectors, seeking depth of experience. Gen Yers, on the other hand are a butterfly generation seeking width of experience which is why you often see them staying in jobs just for a couple of years, (you can hear many of them say, 'I've learnt all there was to learn in this job.'), then moving on for another experience They also claim to know more than their bosses and are happy to tell that to the boss as well! As you can see the two approaches are different, making understanding each other even more challenging.

Under Sourav Ganguly's captaincy, many young players like Harbhajan Singh and Yuvraj Singh flowered. He empowered them and gave them confidence so that they could become match-winners. Irfan Pathan tells of how he was nervous in his first game; the captain threw him the new ball but when he sensed the young man was getting a bit over-awed, he ran up to him to tell him how much he believed in him. Pathan said that if his captain thought he was good enough, he probably was!

At the 1992 World Cup in Australia and New Zealand, Imran Khan had made a public announcement saying he believed that a young man called Inzamam-ul-Huq was the best player of fast bowling. When they got to the semi-final after a scarcely believable, topsy-turvy ride, Inzamam told his captain that he wasn't very keen to play since he wasn't scoring enough runs. Imran told him that he hadn't brought him all the way from Multan to Auckland to drop him. He said he had brought him along because he believed in him and so would play him. The young man played the innings that turned the semi-final around for Pakistan!

Abhishek Jhunjhunwala, who briefly played for the Rajasthan Royals had a similar story to tell about Shane Warne. It was the beginning of the IPL and Abhishek, not one of the stars of the side, was asked by Warne to meet him in London. Not only was he stunned to find that Warne had studied his first class record in detail but was completely blown away when the legend told him, 'Anyone who makes it to my team is a match winner.'[2] The young man came home walking six inches taller that day.

In international teams, as in corporate environments, players make it to the team because they are good enough. A captain or coach needs to make them feel good and happy and create a team climate that supports trust and co-operation. Gautam Gambhir, the Indian opening batsman, felt this need as a player in a team full of batting stars. 'Gary (Kirsten, the coach) told me, he said, how much importance and quality I brought to the side. "You are the one who can anchor the innings, and at the same time you can attack." When you get to know this from a person who has played more than a hundred Tests and who is the coach, then you tell yourself, look, even you are equally important. That has made me comfortable. Earlier no one ever told me what importance I brought to the side. I always used to feel, what I am doing in this side anyone else can do. Now, I realise I have my own role.'

Similarly, if a player is sent out as a pinch hitter, he must believe that it is being done in the team's best interests, that it is not a ploy to push him into a difficult situation. Also, that if he failed in a difficult situation, it wouldn't be held against him. It is the same with a salesman who is asked to flood a retailer to deny competition shelf space and then finds himself under pressure with his collections.

Therefore, the buzz in the dressing room that spells positive energy is largely to do with the climate that the leader creates. Most people in this world don't realise how good they can be and it needs a captain, coach, mentor or boss to encourage wards to challenge themselves all the time, set high goals and grow, as Pathan and many others under Ganguly experienced. John Buchanan calls this 'taking them to places they have never been before'. It's a great line and especially true of players who have come from traditionally weak areas. Who knows how good Mohammad Ashraful of Bangladesh or Steve Tikolo of

Kenya would have been in a different environment under a leader who could have taken them to places they had never been before?

Sometimes, leaders choose team members who are clones of themselves. While a leader may seek comfort in having like-minded characters around him, he is effectively killing variety in thought and debate. Heterogeneity and diversity enriches teams and makes up for flaws inherent to the basic DNA of the team. Even in teams that are lucky to have a Sachin Tendulkar in them, there is a need to have a Dravid, a Sehwag and a Yuvraj Singh. Bowlers work in pairs, so do opening batsmen, Gavaskar and Srikanth for example or, over a longer period, Kumble and Harbhajan. Their differences are what make them complementary. 'Constructed teams' therefore have a greater chance of being ideal teams and more and more companies are proactively trying to build in diversity into their workforce. Diversity without inclusion is meaningless which is why leaders need to ask themselves if they are just as effective with people who are unlike them. Because as Deep Kalra of MakeMyTrip.com put it, 'Team mates who ask you uncomfortable questions are actually your greatest allies.'[3]

Remember though, that captains may not always have the option of a 'constructed' team. They may inherit a lot of dead wood, or to put it simply, players who have only done enough to stay in the team and lack the fervour their skippers may be looking for … or the selectors may not be on the same wavelength as they are, resulting in teams they may not always be comfortable with. Imran resigned twice from the captaincy because he couldn't get the team he wanted. Generally, leaders must seek to construct the teams that they believe work the best for the objective they have in mind while, at the same time, encouraging the players they are stuck with to become as good as they can ever be. Paddy Upton, former coach of the Rajasthan Royals talks about what he considers the non-negotiable selection criterion in making it to any of the teams he coaches. 'For me the criteria number one when we are selecting the top players is that I look at their character, look at what their track record of what they are like in a team environment. If somebody has a questionable character, either through their past history or chequered history or behaviour, if somebody has proven to be in previous teams to be disruptive in a team environment doesn't matter how good they are, does not matter how cheap they are prepared to come and play for us, we put a line through their name. So I will not have overly ego-oriented, narcissistic, self-obsessed, self-important superstars in a team. If you are unfortunate to inherit someone like that, you have got a problem on your hand and if you are foolish enough, greedy enough to choose somebody like that because they have got great numbers or a great history, well then, you have invited a problem onto your hands.'[4]

What really differentiates a leader from the rest (and hopefully his individuality is the reason he's been chosen for the role) is his vision and ability to look beyond what the others see. He is the captain of the ship who sees the calm beyond the storm. Niall Booker says that what a leader needs is perspective, the ability to look at things from a different angle, and if necessary, from someone else's point of view; for example, in the corporate world, the customer's view of a product or service.

The leadership role really begins with the vision, even if it has been largely created by the board of directors or selectors. It's the starting point for the leader, who then communicates it effectively and convincingly to the entire team. It may be as pithy as Manchester United's 'Turning fans into customers' or Nike's 'To bring inspiration and innovation to every athlete in the world' but the leader's job is really to offer a compelling view of the vision to the team. Strategy and goals emerge from this vision and players need to be clear about these goals and the importance of their role, however small, in achieving them. Some time ago in an ad campaign, ICICI Bank said they would open your account before your coffee grew cold. It was a great line but one that had to be transmitted to the bottom of the chain and bought into by everyone. If the person at the branch didn't buy into the theory, he might have *his* coffee while the customer waited for the account to be opened! And so, as teams become bigger and global, leaders need to devise communication strategies that would be both impactful and manageable.

Shane Warne is another who believes very strongly in

each player knowing his role in the team. After leading the Rajasthan Royals to victory in the first IPL in 2008, completely against the odds, he said, 'Things can change so quickly and you need to adapt. We have some set plans to use depending on conditions, whether we bowl short at the end, whether we bowl full, whether we bowl length, slower balls, whatever. You go to a bowler and ask him what he thinks, he might say slower balls and yorkers, so you say okay, switch. Then the players know the field for that. The most important thing is to let the players know what their role is, what they are expected to do. That's where we had an advantage. We were very well prepared and we gave everyone a role and nickname. Graeme Smith was the "Rock at the Top". He batted with Swapnil Asnodkar who was the "Goa Cannon"—go and hit them. We had all these names that the guys loved. A lot of other teams just go out and play and they expect them (the players) to know and they can be dictated to by scoreboard pressure.' Clarity of role and goal is at the heart of execution and absolutely critical now with speed, and therefore getting it right the first time becoming so important.

It is true though that sometimes a player might perceive his role to be insignificant, even unpopular, but if the captain communicates to him that it is critical, he will still do a very effective job of it. It's the captain's job then, to draw the line between being popular or otherwise, and being effective. Nasser Hussain, who did so well for England as a leader, says 'I'd be wary of anyone who's a popular captain because it means the players are getting their own way all the time and getting to do the things they want to do and sometimes you want them to do things they really don't want to do. That's why you have to keep with them so they respect you. You need to keep in mind that you're one of them, and not take yourself too seriously and become some kind of superior being in the dressing room. But you have to get the balance between being one of them and also making sure that when you speak, they listen.'[5]

Hussain was to experience this situation when England came to India under him in 2002 and ran into Sachin Tendulkar in top form. Unable to work out a way of getting him out, they decided to frustrate him by bowling a largely negative outside the leg stump line. The man assigned to do the job was Ashley Giles, a workmanlike spinner who kept things tight. For the next eleven overs he bowled outside the leg stump to Tendulkar, a tactic that drew much criticism. This did keep Tendulkar quiet and ended up frustrating him. 'If you can't bowl him out, bore him out,' the critics said, but as Hussain suggested afterwards, it was a better option than letting Tendulkar get a century! It was a boring job for Giles to do and the key lay in the captain's communication of its importance. If a player knows his role and implements it well, a seemingly small role can become important. At the very least, it can raise a player's self-esteem, as we saw with Gambhir.

Of late, we have come across many organisations

who would like their employees to connect with a higher purpose like a cleaner or healthier India or even a better planet—something larger and beyond the immediate win. One such company with a number of well-known and successful brands selected some employees and sent them on secondment to a new division linked to the higher purpose. The division had the potential to be a game-changer but the employees saw it as a move from a more high-profile brand management job that could show immediate results to a CSR-type assignment that required a huge effort now and results only later. An inspiring vision and authentic communication from a leader would have made getting a buy-in from these managers far easier.

There are times when the team is doing well enough and there are no external threats to keep it on its toes. It is the same situation if the side is a chronic winner, way ahead of competition, like the Australian cricket team was—all through the nineties and early 2000s. Such teams need to be challenged to keep their hunger at an optimum level. Many companies too find their growth rate steadying at a comfortable level, with no perceived need to do anything dramatically different. They face the risk of becoming complacent. Injecting some positive turbulence in teams shakes them up and gets them going.

Positive turbulence is a lovely expression for it means that the leadership is alive to the need of getting ready for what the future might throw up, and getting ready for it in advance. In the mid-nineties, Sri Lanka was a talented side just finding their way in the world. They had players of great skill but not all of them were necessarily athletic enough. That could become an obstacle and so when a new coach arrived, he insisted the team follow a fairly rigorous fitness regimen. It rubbed off on everyone and the new generation Sri Lankan cricketer, a Malinga or a Sangakkara, is possessed of a very different shape from those that took the field earlier. Had the turbulence not been created on time, Sri Lanka may not have become the side that was respected around the world and which first reached the World Cup final in 2007 and then went on to reach three other finals, the World Cup in 2011, the World T20 in 2012 and finally the World T20 in 2014 which they won.

Who Makes a Good Leader

History judges leaders by the quality of the decisions they take. The outcome may not always be beneficial but the boldness and intent behind the decision are what matter. Whether in war, business or sport, decision-making is an integral part of leadership. Those who dilly-dally or fail to take a call are remembered as weak and ineffective leaders. A delay in declaring the innings for example, or a wrong choice of bowler, or a wrong call taken after winning the toss are things that could decide the course of the match. Often, those who choose wisely are the ones that become successful. Pakistan played Australia in the 2009-10 series and had a wonderful opportunity to beat the world champions at home. They had Australia on the ropes with eight wickets down and very few runs in the bank. Instead of going in for the kill, captain Mohammed Yousuf suddenly went defensive, placing fielders on the boundary line and waiting for the batsmen to make a mistake. By the time they did, too many runs had been scored and the game was lost. Yousuf was weighed down by leadership rather than buoyed by it! You see that too in captains who are so afraid of losing that they bat on and on leaving them very little time to bowl the opposition out and win.

This is an important point to study before appointing leaders. Does their own performance dip due to the additional pressure, as might have happened with Sachin Tendulkar, or does their personality bloom as it did with Sourav Ganguly and Virat Kohli? Some people enjoy being leaders; you can see that in their body language, while others are inherently private people, happy to contribute but who find it a burden to take on any responsibility beyond that which they can carry out.

We often ask managers in our corporate sessions to think about whether leadership can be practiced. It is never the same thing but sometimes players on the field can imagine what they would do if they were the captain; what field they would set, or which bowler they would bring on, or whether they would make a substitution. Pep Guardiola, the celebrated football manager says he was always thinking that way as a player at Barcelona, Dhoni got the job in 2007 because Tendulkar, standing at first slip, realised that the young wicket keeper was already thinking like a leader. And Virat Kohli said, before he became captain, that he was always involved in the game, running up to the captain to offer suggestions etc. It came as no surprise that each of these three seemed ready to become the leader because in their minds they had already started thinking like one.

Maybe it is possible for young managers to think about how they would handle a situation or for middle managers to look at a situation from the point of view of a CEO. They would have the advantage of not actually having to take a decision but the thought process would have begun.

Madhabi Puri-Buch, former MD and CEO, ICICI Securities, believes that there are two kinds of leaders: those who believe that 'HR stuff' is an interruption of work and those that believe that it is the most important part of the leader's work. This difference in approach is what, she believes, determines whether the leader flowers or gets bogged down.

It is said that a boardroom where you only hear a single voice is not a very vibrant place. A leader has to be a 'hear-a-holic', with open ears and an open mind since the best ideas can sometimes come from where you least expect them. They could come from one of the 'reserves'; he has little to do, he has no pressure at all and might spot something that has escaped more anxious eyes. He too must be heard. Yet, the final decision has to be the leader's alone. Steve Waugh, in an interview, spoke of the time he had just become captain of Australia. 'As captain, you are in charge and you are responsible for what happens on the field. In a way I was very inexperienced and in that pressure-cooker situation you don't know how you will cope. Initially, I didn't follow my instincts, took advice from too many people. You need to take advice but finally it has to be your own decision. You can't ask people how to run your business—you have to work it out for yourself.'

New leaders, in particular, tend to ask people around them for their view, but rarely is a decision arrived at by consensus. It's also not possible or even desirable for leaders to make everyone happy in the final outcome. Leaders who try to do that rarely achieve success. It requires courage and conviction to take decisions and even more to stand by them. A former Indian cricket captain who tried to involve too many people in deciding strategy also refused to hold himself accountable when he realised that an error in judgement had occurred. Eventually, the buck rests with the leader irrespective of whether the call taken was the right one or not and irrespective of all those who were involved. As Ian Chappell says, 'The Ws and Ls (wins and losses) go against your name.'

A captain can never think 'what if'—what if he had taken another decision, for example, what if he had placed another man in the slips, what if he had hiked his advertising budget, what if he had implemented specific new software. If you have put the opposition in, you have to believe you will win a game even if you don't get instant results; you have to believe in your decision and you have to keep looking ahead however steep and unlikely the outcome.

It was something Shane Warne instilled in his young players during the dramatic ride to victory for the Rajasthan Royals in the inaugural IPL. His mantra to his players was to be positive at all times. Never worry about the situation you are in because that is already upon you, he told them. Instead, ask yourself how you can win from here. Having said that, he then empowered young players to play on the big stage, often drawing performances out of them that they probably didn't think they were capable of themselves! It is an important leadership trait: to believe in your players and give them confidence, for a team that is not empowered is a timid team.

You will find that almost all successful captains, indeed even champions, ask themselves this question: How can you win from here? The starting point is to accept the situation you are in and that is not as easy as it seems because, as we have mentioned, the 'what if' factor is always at the back of your mind. Once you accept the situation you are in and assess what you have left, you can plan an approach that could result in a win. Merely moaning over the situation you are in can never lead to victory.

A leader's positivity can generate hope in a team that could otherwise believe that defeat is imminent. And hope is the strongest weapon a team can possess. Good leaders and champions therefore will always present a situation as do-able rather than impossible; as with the Tendulkar example on how to approach a daunting total in the final of the 2003 World Cup. Or Virat Kohli's strategy to look upon a massive run chase against Sri Lanka as if he was playing two T20 games back to back. Warne says it is important to erase from your mind things that you can no longer do because that will only weigh you down and is a waste of time anyway. Instead, he says, always ask yourself what you can.

This optimism, Imran Khan believes, is a key quality that a leader must possess. He recalled that halfway during the 1992 World Cup, when Pakistan's chances of reaching the final stages were minimal, Intikhab Alam, who was the team manager at the time, came to Imran to ask for his opinion on flight arrangements for the team to fly back home. Imran was surprised and promptly told Intikhab to come back when they actually lost. The rest, as they say, is history.

Sanjay Manjrekar, who had a wonderful series in Pakistan in 1989 and has watched a lot of cricket there, said, 'I never once saw Imran Khan looking towards the stands, or looking elsewhere, He was constantly at us, even if it was a boring Test match. He was always at us … also, I think, not allowing the slightest negativity to creep in … within himself and the rest of the team. Rameez Raja told me how he never ever talked about how good the opposition batsman was. He always talked about how "we" can do it. Even if deep down he knew that the opposition was better, he never let his team mates feel that way.' In fact, a large number of the corporate leaders we spoke to for this book emphasised the importance of this. The 'can-do' attitude is a defining one and one that future leaders must search for within themselves.

A leader would be particularly disadvantaged if he was lacking communication skills. This is not as much to do with fluency and glibness as it is to do with coming through as genuine, and the ability to connect with the heterogenous people who sometimes constitute a team. It is about reaching out to those who are not doing so well. It is about trusting the team and being seen as someone who can be trusted.

Communication skills are important for entrepreneurs as well and not something that they invest time in, says Ronnie Screwvala.[6] You could be a genius and have a great idea but you need to communicate that effectively as well—to your team, your associates and even your investors.

When he appeared on our show *Masterstrokes* on CNBC, Sourav Ganguly said that good leaders got their decisions right seven times out of ten. Rather modestly he gave himself a five but said that even if he was wrong the team trusted him and believed that he made mistakes while trying to do his best for the team. No wonder he was credited with changing the fortunes of the team as captain! It is a wonderful position for the leader to reach and highlights why generating trust is one of the fundamental tenets of leadership.

However, the extent of communication, like good spices in a curry, needs to be just right! Ian Chappell believes that if captains over-communicate it may prove ineffective and so he left speech-making for the big and important occasions when it would have the desired impact. E. A. S. Prasanna too remembers Tiger Pataudi as being a captain of few words. A nod or mere shake of the head from Tiger was enough, says Prasanna.

Tiger Pataudi, with his royal lineage and Oxford education, was much younger than, and socially quite far removed from, many of the other players from the team. Tiger was made captain of India at the young age of 21. In fact, he captained in 41 of the 46 Tests that he played. Tiger could never have been one of the boys as Dhoni is today. Yet his charisma, quite like Imran Khan's, made him a respected captain. By contrast, Western teams are far more egalitarian. Mukul Deoras sums it up by saying, 'Western leaders depend more on clarity of two-way communication and implicit delegation. Eastern leadership is perhaps a lot more feudal. They depend on clarity of instruction and alignment.'[7]

'Many companies in India are promoter-owned which brings a very strong personal leadership style where, typically, the thinking and the main decision-making is done at the very top and the rest is more or less execution. Even if it is at a very high level, it is still execution. There is a very well-defined area of authority and outside of that you go back to the boss. In our system (which is far more egalitarian), you come back to the team,' observes Marten Pieters.[8]

Like the Indian vs. expat issue, the leader from inside vs. the outsider issue has also been discussed at great length. Mukul Deoras believes that an outsider is important if we believe that the team is incapable of thinking outside its set pattern and/or needs competencies which are not available within the team. Hence the reason for looking at overseas coaches, for example, in Indian cricket.

Sandip Das has an interesting take on this which seems to justify Ian Chappell's thinking. He says, 'Most mothers complain that their children suffer from "mother deafness" because they are constantly chiding their children and the kids do not seem to respond ... then fathers say the same thing and suddenly things happen. CEOs feel similarly about CEO deafness. You could be saying wonderful new things to your people and the response could be frustratingly lukewarm. Yet one fine day, you get a CEO of another company to come in to talk to your people. When he leaves, they will rave about the wonderful things he said, although you might have been saying them for years inside the company. So occasionally, it helps to get that little intervention from outside, for changes and for impact. It is a symptom of freshness, new perspective and arguably, more perceived objectivity.'[9]

'Tiger' Tyagarajan, who has spent many years with GE, known as a training ground for so many global leaders, says that GE has a systematic process of grooming future leaders. When these leaders do take over, their team accepts them more easily. It is almost expected that they take over. Australia tends to do that and when one captain retires, the identity of his successor is rarely a mystery. The continuity helps. Australia had only six captains between 1985 and 2017, whereas Pakistan might have gone through those many in a few months some years ago! Tiger believes that outside leaders need to be parachuted in only to organisations where there is no process in place or 'when there is no credit given to mentors or there is a lack of self-confidence and security among current leaders who then don't hire people better than them and who could take their job.'[10]

True leaders like challenges so that they can prove themselves in tough situations. So although a crisis or change or downturn might find the team in turmoil, leaders are willing to give it a go as a personal challenge. Some coaches would rather coach a Sri Lanka or a New Zealand, which are good but have a lot more scope for improvement, than a team like Australia that was on top for a while. Some others might believe that *staying* on top is almost as difficult a challenge. It is an interesting question for leaders to ask themselves. Which team would you rather lead? A team that's been number one for ten years or another that is number six, has limited resources, but has the potential to make it big? In a public forum the answer would be obvious and hence the need to ask yourself!

Inevitably, all attention on the field drifts towards the leader. Teams that are down look to him for direction and would rather see a calm captain than one who is seen to be chewing his nails or gesturing all over the place. Mark Taylor was known for his unflappable nature and it was impossible to know by watching him whether his team was struggling or cruising. So too with Mahendra Singh Dhoni. The opposition should be led to believe that the leader might still have a few aces up his sleeve and, certainly, that he isn't going to give up easily. A young captain like Virat Kohli is different in that his face tends to be a mirror to his thoughts but within a year of becoming captain, he had already talked of the need to preserve his energy and not waste it in on-field displays of aggression. It is appropriate therefore that Ian Chappell talks about the need for a captain to even out his own emotions whatever his own performance. 'Don't yell on the field,' he says, 'because that sends out a signal to the opposition.'

A captain's own performance can be an irritant to the job unless that can be effectively separated from leadership. Some years ago when still captain of India, Sourav Ganguly said he had told Rahul Dravid, who he thought would be India's next captain, about the importance of taking decisions as captain whether or not he is getting runs. 'If you mix up the two roles you are in trouble,' he said.

An optimistic leader, one who displays confident body language, can also be the glue for a team in a crisis. Teams rally around such leaders. John Buchanan's theory of the coach being redundant may hold for a winning team, but we believe that a team in trouble must have a visibly hands-on leader, like Rudy Giuliani (mayor of New York) was during 9/11. Or a team must have a leader who possesses the quality of leadership that Bharat Puri displayed during the 'worms in chocolate' affair. When you have inspirational leaders taking on a situation, players can end up playing for the captain, which is not a bad thing really.

When Leaders Are Tested

Teams sometimes go into a losing streak and end up getting white-washed in the series. It is something we are seeing increasingly and often this is not due to poor performance alone but because morale has taken a beating as well. Teams end up taking the field convinced that they cannot win; they look around at each other and wonder which of them is going to be a match-winner. If on tour they start thinking of being home, of being in familiar places. At such times matches tend to be lost before they actually are. Good players don't become bad players overnight, which explains the saying, class is permanent, form is temporary. The most natural reaction of a leader would be to focus on improving the performance but this is hardly likely without morale being boosted. Often it is a re-injection of self-belief that brings the team back on track.

Sometimes leaders need to take tough calls like giving negative feedback or dropping a player. Such decisions, however painful, can neither be avoided nor delayed.

Rahul Dravid faced public outcry when, as captain in Pakistan, he declared the innings with Tendulkar not out on 194. However, that was a decision that needed to be taken if the team was to win. In our corporate programmes, we ask leaders what they would have done in a similar situation because leaders will be forced at times to choose between the individual and the team. It is not easy and it needs a tough captain to take tough decisions, to put the team ahead of an individual landmark. Eventually, the leader who puts the team first tends to be respected.

We saw that twice during Test matches in England. The first was in 1997 at Manchester, when the Australian captain Mark Taylor made a seemingly puzzling decision. The conditions were overcast, the pitch was green and it was a toss crying to be won so that the opposition could be asked to bat first. However, Taylor knew that on that surface, spinners would come into the game on day four and five, and so, to allow Shane Warne to bowl in the fourth innings and try and win Australia the Test, they needed to bat first. Steve Waugh writes, 'When Tubby (Taylor) returned and announced he had won the toss and elected to bat, disbelief swept the room. On the surface, his decision appeared foolhardy and a massive gamble but he had backed his gut.... A captain needs to see the bigger picture.' It is an aspect young leaders need to be aware of as they rise through the ranks. A captain needs to see the bigger picture.

In the 2002 Test series between India and England,

India went to Leeds one down with two games to play. It was a blustery day, the pitch was a touch damp, rain was in the air, and it was again a win-toss-bowl-first pitch. But India's captain Sourav Ganguly backed his side to combat the conditions and batted first. It was a vote of confidence in the team and they rallied to the call. Once the conditions were conquered, runs were made quite freely and India drew the series. The boldness of the decision and the ability of the team to back it make it one of India's finest test wins ever.

England's former captain Andrew Strauss, when appointed as the head of the England cricket team, demonstrated this ability to see the bigger picture, something English cricket's leadership had struggled to do, caught up as they were with their loyalties to their counties and the need to preserve a traditional cricket culture. After seeing England's pathetic, outdated performance at the World Cup, he realised that players needed to get exposure to what the rest of the world was doing, to see for themselves what the best were doing. And that limited overs cricket was the future. The new coach, Trevor Bayliss, had a track record of success in limited overs cricket but had little to show in long form cricket. And, more important, Strauss allowed, even encouraged, players who weren't playing test cricket in May to look for contracts in T20 leagues around the world. England became competitive in limited overs cricket very quickly thereafter and even made the final of the World T20 in March 2016.

So leaders need to take tough decisions during tough times. During the 2008-09 recession, companies floundered. Executives who were used to luxuries during boom times, were suddenly asked to cut back costs, forgo bonuses, even move into smaller houses. It's difficult to ask people for more while giving less. One way of getting around things is for the leader to set the example. Niall Booker at HSBC said, 'If you are asking people to cut back, you need to be seen to do the same. I got rid of the Mercedes and had a Honda Accord as the company car in India. People need to trust you.' In a similar vein, Barry Richards said of Ian Chappell, 'He never asked people to do something he wouldn't do himself. He didn't believe in a night watchman and wanted a batsman to go out himself. But then he did the same when it was his turn.' On chartered flights within India for the national team, the captain was entitled to a business class seat. But Dhoni always sat at the back and gave his seat to a fast bowler because he was aware they needed the comfortable seat more than he did. Many leaders say the right things but few walk the talk. Authentic leaders earn the respect of their teams and even their competitors.

There is a feeling that Indian managers generally shy away from giving timely and honest feedback. This is because Indians treat feedback as criticism and don't take it as constructive feedback that will help them improve. Indians are also people-oriented, often putting people ahead of the task. This shows in the way we are so poor with constructive culling, often letting non-performers continue well beyond their sell-by date. It helps nobody, because a leader's skill lies as much in picking a player at the right time as in letting him go at the required moment. We are sentimental people and we tend to hang on to our good-byes and while the intention can be noble at a personal level, it is not a great team-building tactic, for there is a fear of accumulating non-performing people assets.

A. S. Ramchander, Executive Director at Castrol India at one time, told us, 'Within an organisation, honesty in giving feedback is often avoided in order to be polite. The evaluator (the one giving feedback) will have credibility only if he is honest. Yet specifics are missed out and the once-a-year performance appraisal confuses the juniors.'[11]

However, Indian managers seem to have an inherent advantage in managing uncertainty as well as diversity. As Jerry Rao puts it, 'Indians are used to cultural diversity from a young age. Since our infrastructure is so bad, when things go wrong, they know how to improvise. They develop the smarts that, say, people working in Singapore, where everything works like clockwork, don't develop. We also have an irrational government that takes abrupt policy decisions that could upset your cost calculation and competitive advantage. Such abrupt decision-making is required in hi-tech industries as well, though not due to the external environment. One learns to adapt and put multiple bets on the possible outcomes. Indians are used to dealing with labour unions who can have a completely different agenda. It helps you realise that there could be another point of view.'[12]

This was amply demonstrated by Lalit Modi when, in a span of a mere three weeks, he successfully moved the second IPL tournament to South Africa after the Central government expressed its inability to guarantee sufficient security-cover for the players in the wake of elections being announced at around the same time as the IPL. To move a tournament of such magnitude, involving such complicated logistics and international participation at such short notice says a lot about Lalit Modi's guts as well as his decision-making. To many it would have seemed an impossible move but as always, in difficulty there lurks an opportunity. By producing an impeccable IPL 2, Modi produced a global Indian brand that may not have been possible had it remained in India. So there it is, in times of crisis, you need a hands-on leader who is looking beyond apparent difficulties.

The Best Player Need Not Make the Best Captain

It is good that Imran Khan did not suffer from insecurity, or else the cricketing world would have missed players like Wasim Akram and Waqar Younis. Imran always put Pakistan first and was very secure himself, so he didn't mind picking young players who, in a few years, would actually become better than him, for his skills would decline with age. He also believed in leading from the front and so, when his fast-bowling skills had significantly declined during the World Cup campaign of 1992, he moved up to number three in the batting order. The captain was making a statement there.

Imran was also aware, as all good captains should, that if his younger players grew to become outstanding players, he would win more matches as captain because, as we said earlier, the wins and losses go against a captain's name. And so he ensured that Waqar Younis was not allowed to become anything other than a genuine fast bowler and he held Wasim Akram's hand till Akram became the champion cricketer that he is now recognised as.

The story goes that as a young player extraordinarily gifted, Akram could bowl every ball in the game but hadn't yet learnt the art of thinking a batsman out, didn't therefore know which ball to bowl when and to whom. Imran, as captain, was now well past his best as a bowler but still knew what to bowl to get a batsman out. And so, ball by ball, Imran would guide Akram and as he himself said, a day came when he was at mid-off and the game seemed to have stopped. He looked at his bowler, who was at the top of his run-up and said, 'What happened?' 'Skipper, you haven't told me which ball to bowl' was apparently Akram's response.

Imran could do this because he was a secure leader. He had the experience, but no longer the expertise needed. Akram had all the skill but didn't yet possess the experience. The combination though, using the best both had to offer, was brilliant. And this combination of experience and expertise has great possibilities in industry where technology makes senior managers less informed compared to the youngsters entering the work force but allows them to mould the knowledge bursting through the younger lot. So instead of conflict between generations, can companies tap the invaluable strengths present and use it to mutual benefit? This combination of experience and expertise is something good teams must employ.

What starts early in life with the best student in class being made the class monitor continues till much later with the best salesman being made sales manager or the star batsman becoming captain. The law of natural progression is followed the world over, in spite of it being proved wrong over and over again. Star performers are supreme individualists, totally focused on themselves and their craft. In a sense, their obsession with themselves is what defines their genius.

A leader, on the other hand, needs to think beyond himself and ahead of everyone else. He needs to relate to people whose talent does not match his own and needs to spend time with players who are not performing as well as him.

While doing so, a leader must also answer a simple question: Do I spend more time with people who are in form and delivering as they are meant to, or do I spend more time with under-performers who need some hand-holding?

One reason outstanding talents don't always make

the best leaders is that they tend to weigh everyone in the same scales they weigh themselves in and so, sometimes are unable to understand the limited capability, even the insecurity, of another player. As one international player said to us about his captain, 'Has he ever known what it is to go to bed wondering if he will make the team the next day?' In fact, Sachin Tendulkar admitted to us in the interview we did with him that his fast bowler Javagal Srinath told him that he tended to measure people in the way he measured himself.

Understanding a person therefore, is critical, because you still need that person on the team and also get the best out of them. Michael Holding, as we have seen, said something similar when we asked him about his captain Clive Lloyd. There was a feeling that you didn't really need to do much with that great West Indies side since everyone knew their role and they were the most awesome bunch of players to take the field. (In years to come, New Zealander Chris Cairns would say that his mother could captain Australia!) But as Holding said, 'Lloydy took the trouble to understand that we were all different and because he respected us, we respected him.'

The other reason the best performer need not make the best leader, is that leadership requires a whole new set of skills. An outstanding software programmer, for example, caught up in the daily affair with his machine, might never learn to handle people; a very good shop floor manager might not possess the communication skills to lead a less homogeneous group. There are many professions and job profiles today—lawyers, research scientists, IT engineers, creative heads in advertising agencies where people are great assets as individual contributors but not quite leadership material. In a world where leadership is associated with the size of the team you manage or the territory you oversee, these people feel left out if they are not made people managers. Making them leaders could be a double whammy—you lose a great contributor and get a poor leader instead! 'You have to give them a great career path and power them, open up the door and let them do what they love doing. Recognize their brilliance but make sure they understand their own weaknesses,' suggests Pramod Bhasin.[13]

Understanding that the qualities that brought you so far are not the ones that will necessarily take you forward is an adjustment that many fail to make. So, teams might be better off looking at those who may appear to be less-gifted individuals in the practice of a sport or function, if they possess the ability to bring the best out of the team.

The need to have both skills, that of a performer and also being able to understand the capability of others, is therefore a combination that few possess. As Madhabi Puri-Buch told us, 'The leader must also come with impeccable credentials. Today's youngsters, in particular, will not respect a leader if he/she is not a performer in his/her own right.' Her philosophy is that a leader can command respect only if he is able to say, 'If you can't do it, I will.'[14]

Genius also has a twin brother in ego and success

only strengthens the bond between the siblings. Saugata Gupta feels that greed and a lack of humility are the two main reasons why leaders fall. 'Sometimes, leaders get caught up in pet projects. You should be able to judge things from a distance. Often, there aren't people who will tell the leader that he is wrong. It is lonely at the top.'

Leaders Come with a Shelf-Life

While discussing leadership issues we often talk about different situations needing, almost demanding, different kinds of leaders. Wartime generals are required for inspired action, for taking the bull by the horns. Peace time managers are brought in when you need to sustain a campaign. Neither of those skills is superior, as seen in the case of Winston Churchill who was rejected by the British electorate when the need to rebuild, after the euphoria of the victory in war, became paramount.

Post the match-fixing issue at the turn of the century, Indian cricket needed a flamboyant, inspirational leader, not just to carry the team along but to convince the fans that they were out there doing their best. Sourav Ganguly was the right man and he was wonderful in transforming India from a defensive, uncertain side, especially overseas, into one that could win anywhere. By doing this, he brought the people back into the game and supporting the national side. In fact, you could say cricket in India recovered almost too quickly from that match-fixing affair!

By 2005, India were respected around the world but Ganguly's own form was taking a dip and there was a feeling he might be a touch insecure. When the time came for a change, India found an outstanding peacetime manager in Rahul Dravid whose style was rather more low-key. Without making headlines for his leadership, he took India to victory in the West Indies in 2006, for the first time in 35 years, and in England in 2007, for the first time in 21 years. Ganguly and Dravid were the right people at the right time; one a wartime leader, the other a peacetime manager.

So too were Anil Kumble and Mahendra Singh Dhoni. Kumble, with his dignity and stature and compulsive work ethic, was the right man for a potentially draining tour of Australia in 2008. The small-town Dhoni was just about perfect to lead new India and its aspirations which he could understand better than anyone else. And Virat Kohli seems to possess the attributes that the go-getting generation transforming India can relate to.

This sense of timing is critical in industry as well, as we have seen in the next generation of the Bajaj family and in the trend-setting Ambanis. Dhirubhai was the pioneer, starting small, recognising opportunity and building the company. As India changed and began taking its place in the world, Reliance found that Mukesh Ambani, with his global outlook and ambition was the man for the occasion. Maybe it is purely an academic issue whether both father and son would have done equally well if the roles and timing, were reversed but Reliance certainly benefited enormously from having the right people leading it at the right time.

Another example that illustrates this quite vividly was Australia's resurgence in the late eighties. In the mid-eighties, plagued by the mistrust that arose between the former Packer players and those that backed the establishment, and grievously injured by the rebel tours to South Africa, Australia had hit rock bottom in the world of cricket. Much to their discomfiture they were even being beaten by their little cousin, New Zealand. Their captain, Kim Hughes, had tearfully resigned the captaincy.

Almost by default then, the mantle was delivered to a tough, stubborn back-room boy called Allan Border. With coach Bob Simpson and with a lot of help from the selectors (showing perhaps, the importance of everyone in the management sticking together) Border and Australia decided to rebuild on the 'attitude first' principle. They selected mentally tough, proud cricketers, sometimes ahead of more gifted players who may not have had the right attitude. You could see that in the selection of people like Steve Waugh and David Boon who once, famously, asked for an injury to be stitched up on the field rather than leaving it and giving away a psychological advantage.

Border's philosophy in Test cricket was understandably, geared towards not losing for he had seen enough of it. Australia battled hard, fielded brilliantly and were gritty rather than flair cricketers. By and by, the victories started to arrive. The World Cup of 1987 and the Ashes in 1989 had been important landmarks but Australia still couldn't beat the West Indies. Border had been part of too many losing campaigns against them.

By 1993-94, it became apparent that Border was coming to the end of his career. The team was fairly stable now but the big win against the West Indies was still eluding them. Australia's selectors then took the tough call and decided that Mark Taylor would replace Allan Border as captain on his retirement. Taylor was as different from Border as possible. He had always been captain of his side, enjoyed it and always looked to win. It helped him that he had inherited a fairly stable side but the mindset still needed to change. With Taylor's forward-looking, aggressive approach, Australia beat the West Indies for the first time in the Caribbean in 1995.

With Border and Taylor, and Ganguly and Dravid, it was the right man in charge at the right time. Had the order been reversed, Taylor in the mid-eighties and Border thereafter, Australia may not have been as well served.

In management too, leaders who steer companies out of tight situations with prudent controls and tight spending, could find it difficult to lead the ship when giant investments fuelled by optimism are the need of the hour. You need grit in one situation and vision in another. You need someone to count the paise in one situation and someone to invest the big rupees in another.

Not surprisingly, therefore, leaders have a shelf-life

too. Ian Chappell thinks there is a voice inside that tells you when it is time to go. There comes a time when the speeches seem tired, the new ideas seem familiar and the tricks become repetitive. Sometimes pressure takes its toll and the leader can feel spent; that could start affecting his performance as a player. It is important to remember though that there is no formula for determining shelf-life. Jose Mourinho was thought good enough for two years at Chelsea, indeed two-three years in one job seems to be his best bet, but Alex Ferguson and Arsene Wenger seemed to go on and on for Manchester United and Arsenal. Ganguly did the job for five years while Dravid thought his time had come in two. This is something that those who appoint leaders need to keep an eye out for. That is why, as with players, leaders need to be picked and culled at the right time.

Who is a Good Leader?

One who:

- makes the team add up to more than the sum of the parts;
- has vision and communicates to inspire;
- manages team climate;
- is trusted and respected;
- backs the team at all times;
- is approachable and understands the team; empowers the team, creates more leaders;
- takes them to places they have never been before;
- is open, flexible, honest and a hear-a-holic;
- is positive, optimistic;
- is courageous in decision-making; always works in the interest of the team;
- is secure, willing to surround himself with people better than himself;
- can accept responsibility and give credit;
- serves as team glue.

What Price—Winning?

Play with respect. Win with grace.

—Roger Federer

There are always a few people who come up to us after a live session is over; after all the questions about handling failure, handling difficult bosses and then, invariably, who the best cricket captain India has ever produced is, have been publicly handled (or sometimes dodged!) in the Q&A that follows. The last question is particularly tricky since the person asking the question inevitably has a name in mind and makes it obvious that it is the answer he would like to hear! But the people who come after the Q & A is over, are quiet, gentle people. They come and ask philosophical questions that force you to think. Does everyone need to win, they ask? What if I am not a Sachin Tendulkar? Is winning worth achieving if you need to pay a heavy price? Basically, they want to know, is winning everything?

You would recall that, early in the book, we have said that according to us, winning is being the best that you can possibly be. The purpose therefore is the pursuit of excellence and the assumption is that the means are fair. There is no doubt that today individuals and corporations are driven to win, more than ever before. What is often under question is the commitment to excellence and the desire to win without compromising on the means.

Cheating has always been a small but dark part of sport whether it is diving in the penalty area or pushing a ball into the goal with your hand or claiming a catch when you know the ball hasn't hit the bat. One of the reasons it isn't criticized enough is that increasingly in sport, the influencers have been perpetrators in the past and justify it as happening in the heat of battle. It is seen as a fair trick to play, as being shrewd. It runs the risk of influencing society, especially to a generation that looks up to sport (even if for the right reasons most times!)

It can be worse. There are always the odd bad eggs in many disciplines, some caught out immediately, others eventually. Match-fixing, doping (occasionally, like in the case of Russian athletes, with full sanction of the authorities), corruption and bribery have proliferated more in recent times. Greed, which is at the heart of it, takes away from the purity of winning. And when greed becomes all-consuming, excellence becomes secondary. Look around and you will find many organizations that are financially very successful but compromised in their commitment to excellence. It's a strange situation when mediocrity thrives and is given a veneer of respectability on account of its sellability. It becomes particularly apparent in businesses like media, educational institutes, telecom companies etc. where your power comes from being one of the few to be able to offer limited admissions or airwaves. Profit becomes the top priority by some distance and excellence then is purely optional. Is winning worth having when your reputation is poor and your credibility low? We think not.

> How will a sport survive if its finest values—of honest effort, persistence, a respect for the rules, the acceptance of defeat—itself become redundant? How will a sport survive if everyone is cheating at every stage?
>
> —Rahul Dravid in the
> M. A. K. Pataudi memorial lecture

Greed can also make people take undue risk. Success is so heady that it makes people feel invincible. Lance Armstrong blamed this feeling of invincibility for his involvement in the doping scandal that eventually led to his downfall. There could be little doubt that Tiger Woods who like Armstrong defined his sport, felt that way too with his many escapades. The by-product of this apparent invincibility could be shattering as both discovered as indeed did Hansie Cronje many years earlier. Cronje's is the most fascinating case; a powerful, inspiring leader who produced a band of devoted followers, was one of the personalities most looked-up to in cricket but who had a fatal infatuation with money and used his power, and apparent invincibility, to seek it. He leaves behind a valuable lesson to those, especially to corporate leaders, that get carried away by their own power.

Greed could drive people and organizations to bankruptcy as well. The fall of Lehmann Brothers, Enron, Kingfisher and Sahara shows what greed can lead to. Old-timers like N. R. Narayana Murthy therefore insist that values come first, performance second. Long-term team culture cannot be compromised for short-term gains and that is what a leader must have the courage to do at all times. Paddy Upton, who played a major role in building the Rajasthan Royals team speaks of how it wasn't enough for his teams to have good players. They needed to be good team players with good character. It must have hurt Upton and Dravid that, unknown to them, hidden amongst those in their team were the very people they were so keen to jettison.

It is not uncommon to see organizations that don't invest in building a good work culture ending up becoming profitable but unhappy places to work. Unhappy people either leave or don't feel motivated to give their best and so this exploitative strategy is at best a short-term strategy and one that will not make winning sustainable. Strange as it may sound, even individuals can be successful and yet unhappy. Their success might have come at the expense of their health or their family life. No doubt that in order to achieve something one needs to sacrifice something but often the price is so high that winning just doesn't seem worth it. Or maybe, it leaves you in a position where you can't enjoy your success.

Most successful people say the best career decision is one that allows you to follow your passion, do what you love to do. In our system, many students often get pushed into making career choices based on the dreams of their family. Young people travel and live alone, away from the support of their families. They are not equipped to handle the pressure of expectations that gets further intensified by the loans and sacrifices of family members. The so-called successful Kota model of 'Excel or get left behind' is now being questioned after more than fifty-seven young lives have been lost in the last five years. Sometimes young people aspire to join their dream companies but having made it there discover that they are uncaring, indifferent workplaces where they feel unappreciated or unfulfilled. This is the fastest and easiest way to kill the dreams and the drive of young talent and push them to only think about themselves and become poor team players.

The most significant feature of the last decade has been the abundance of opportunities in almost all sectors of business. Sport, as much of a business today as medicine or education, has also thrown up opportunities, career options and revenue sources for athletes and the organizations that run sport. However, today's world suffers from a strange paradox where opportunities are aplenty but the fear of disruption leaves everyone vulnerable. By the looks of it, winning seems to have become relatively short-lived. Brands and companies too appear to flirt with winning rather than embrace it in a tight hug. 'The average tenure of a CEO has gone down to four years and companies don't get to teenagership,' says D. Shivakumar while quoting industry statistics. In quite the same manner, earlier sports icons were few, stayed in the public memory for a long time and were only talked about for their records or sporting achievement. Today, the media has ensured that there are many known names and recognizable faces. Athletes are seen modelling in ads as much as they are seen performing in matches but not everyone remains in the public eye for very long.

Earlier, people from larger cities, or more affluent and privileged sections of society, were the ones who got to know of opportunities and therefore got to grab them. The arrival of Mahendra Singh Dhoni as captain or Abdul Kalam as President signalled the arrival of change in India. The widespread penetration of the internet has ensured democratisation of knowledge and a level playing field. Whether it is a cricket or football team or an IIT or an IIM, the large chunk of talent is coming from smaller towns. Fairly new Indian companies like Patanjali or Micromax have stood up to established multinationals. Today's winner looks like a confident, almost brash *desi*, not a convent-educated, westernized affluent guy.

Opportunities and options in business has meant that money is not the only driver in career decisions. It continues to remain important to youngsters who, unlike our generation, are not savings-driven but instead are caught up with managing their EMIs. For the talented in this generation, money is important but not a worry. Their bigger consideration is to find appreciation and fulfillment at the workplace. And the key to that is in having a fair and appreciative boss. Managers in their forties, sandwiched between bright Gen Yers and experienced seniors find themselves challenged from both ends. Insecure middle managers, youngsters say, are either credit-snatchers or idea-killers. This seems to be a top reason for attrition and a poor way for bosses to get ahead as well. Increasingly leaders will need to be assessed on how well they can retain and nurture talent. Only then will they be seen as winners. What they say about people joining companies but leaving bosses seems true.

Social media has made it easy for individuals and brands to become famous quickly. But as quickly as you can make a name, your reputation can get dented overnight, as Nestle discovered. Nestle took a hit of Rs. 450 crore as it destroyed 30,000 tonnes of noodles. As the news of lead in Maggi spread like wild fire, Nestle reported a loss of Rs. 64 crores, its first in three decades.

So, has the concept of winning changed over the years? Is today's generation looking at winning differently? Earlier brands were built to last, to be profitable. Now start-ups have at all times one eye on valuation. They are happy to take the business to a certain level and equally happy to sell it to someone who will take it further. 'Not everyone is looking to build an Amazon,' thinks Sandip Das.[1] External funding helps companies acquire customers quickly but could you call it a loyal customer base? If the answer is that you are not sure, does it qualify as winning?

'There is no copybook way to succeed, there's no Rahul Dravid model anymore to winning,' observes Saugata Gupta. 'If you are a risk-taker, there are many more opportunities for short-term wins. Sometimes a series of short-term wins adds up to more than a focused long term win,' he suspects, seeing the new generation of serial entrepreneurs and investors.[2] Even in the IPL, eight wins are enough to take you through. Teams therefore don't stress as much about a few losses as long as they have the required wins.

True, there are many more paths to winning than before and new ways to look at winning. Experience and grey hair are giving way to disruptive ideas and go-getters who are willing to back themselves and their ideas. CEOs are getting younger and while there's no substitute for hard work, timeframes are collapsing. So if it took sixty years for an HUL to set up their formidable distribution network, it took ITC only twenty to achieve the same. And Flipkart managed that reach in five years and through a very different process. Since freelancing and outsourcing have become very common the idea of loyalty has undergone a change as well.

Loyalty is, increasingly, towards the role and skill rather than the organization. So you could be a digital marketer but work for a string of companies without actually being on their rolls. Quite like a T20 player who plays in the IPL during April and May and then goes on to play in the Big Bash and then the Caribbean Premier League not to speak of similar tournaments in Dhaka and Dubai. He moves from team to team but at all times strives to be the best No. 3 batsman or leg spinner in the team. He could be a great team player without having a lasting association with any of the teams. And since he comes with a well-publicised price tag at every team he plays for, his idea of winning is probably to justify that price tag through his performance. No wonder Sourav Ganguly believes that it's a tougher job to captain an IPL team than to captain India. There was also a time when wearing the national team colours was the ultimate, even the only, way to achieve pride and glory. You ask a player today and he will tell you that a hefty cheque from the franchise is not a bad option even if you don't win a test cap!

So the paths to winning might have altered, the symbols of success might look changed but the overall concept of winning, that it is a byproduct of the pursuit of excellence, remains constant. Winning is a journey to explore your potential to the fullest, to discover how good you can be. And so you can be a winner regardless of whether someone else's performance looks better or worse than your own. You can be a winner only if you have achieved this potential by just and fair means, not by cheating or exploiting another. Success is not worth a penny if it leaves you spent, bitter or guilty. There is nothing quite like winning if it leaves you satisfied and fulfilled, refreshed and ready to scale new peaks.

What Sport Has Taught Me

Anand Mahindra

No matter how blessed you are, life cannot be only about winning. Which is why sport must be an essential part of our lives. Sport teaches us not just how to celebrate victory, but how to cope with, and conquer loss. And without that skill, we would find it hard to survive.

Niall Booker

You learn when to play safe and when to take risks.

Jerry Rao

Sport has taught me humility. I didn't excel in sport though I would have liked to. I got very high marks. MBAs and the like can have intellectual arrogance. But sport taught me that there are other ways to look at things, others can be better than you in other ways. Maybe you are not all that hot.

Mukul Deoras

Never give up, matches are not won or lost till the last ball. Also, one person alone cannot win, nor do everything. Each of us has a valuable role to play.

Bharat Puri

Winning is a habit. Cultivate it but never forget that you win some, you lose some. Be humble in victory and gracious in defeat.

Neeraj Garg

Never to give up, you can never be sure who will win, the biggest guy needn't always win. People only remember no.1 so you should try to be no.1 even on a small metric—so set a creative goal.

Vivek Kudva

Because we usually enjoy sport, the fact that we may lose more often than we win, does not mean that we stop playing the sport or trying!

Saugata Gupta

Sports teaches you about teams, winning and losing, discipline, tactics. That you can contribute to a team, but can't do without others

Deep Kalra

Teamwork (soccer and relays), perseverance (swimming and running alone), discipline (all) and the zest to win.

Nitin Paranjpe

The price you pay for even a momentary lapse can be very significant

Marten Pieters

There are 6 players in a volleyball team. If you have 5 brilliant players but one is not good, you can never win a good game. Similarly in business, if you have a very strong team but one or two individuals don't contribute, you need to change them to optimize the team.

A. S. Ramchander

There is always a second chance.

The best performer is not always the leader. For being a team leader, working with and motivating the team is lot more important than raw talent and skills.

Sandip Das

Average teams can have miraculous wins with belief and leadership. Spectacular teams can flatter to deceive, when self is put before the team.

Satya Nadella

I remember learning one of my first leadership lessons on that team. There was an incident where I was bowling and wasn't performing at my best. My captain at that time took over from me and got the team a breakthrough and then he handed the bowling back to me and I did go onto taking the most wickets in that inning. I remember being stunned when he did that. It would have made more sense for him to continue, but it left an impression on me. I think that's an important leadership lesson that I've carried with me, in terms of how leaders build confidence around their team and empower people to believe in their own abilities.

The Last Word
What It Means to Be a Team Player

Even as a child I was drawn to team sports. The fun and friendships shared with team mates, the joy and sorrow of winning or losing together, the ability to get along with others, are things familiar to anyone who has played even the most basic level of any team sport. As I graduated to higher levels of cricket and spent a lot of time travelling and playing, I discovered many more aspects to being a team player.

Apart from enjoying one's own performance, it is highly motivating to participate in the very special process of taking the team to another level. Being in high-pressure situations along with teammates and working towards strategies to counter the opposition can be hugely satisfying, even more so when you actually succeed. Team sport not only provides the space for individual growth but also an opportunity to reach out to those who are not doing that well. And believe me, success is a strangely cyclical phenomenon that all players experience. In any team, there will be people in good form and others who struggle. Very often then, especially if you are doing well, there is an opportunity to contribute to someone else's success, and experience the pride of seeing your team mate grow as a person. On the other hand, you might be in bad form, but the team still wins, and you have something to be happy about. The beauty of being part of a team is the security it offers along with the realisation that it's not about you alone.

Playing cricket in India means you will have to face the diversity that our country offers. Playing alongside individuals with different abilities and backgrounds teaches you to accept and respect differences without either being intimidated or being snobbish. The dressing room is a place filled with laughter and humour, with everyone pulling each other's leg. But different people have different sensibilities and not everyone can go with the joke to the same extent. When you spend so much time together you learn where to draw the line. You recognise the fine line between laughing with others and laughing *at* others. Apart from humour, there are so many memories and stories that bind a team together. And winning brings out the best in people, makes them more giving as well as more forgiving. If you notice, all this talk about the great team spirit that defined the Australian team through the late Nineties and early 2000s coincided with their hugely successful run. I am a great believer in the Power of Winning.

I have noticed that good team-players view success very differently from the rest. They are motivated without really worrying about credit. That's not always easy. Anyone who has fielded at short leg knows what a thankless job it is, besides being risky. You put your body on the line, have to work damn hard and may have nothing to show for it. When given that position, there are those who are reluctant to put in the hard work, hoping that they will be made to field in another position the next time round, and there are others who give it their best and actually become specialists.

One can empathise with batsmen who come in to bat at number five, six or seven in a one-day match. They have a limited number of balls to make an impact and show their worth. If they are under pressure to retain their position, they are tempted to take the high-risk option of hitting big shots that may not be in the team's interest at that stage of the match.

Situations like diving or fielding, in which you put your body at risk, or where you are required to play a role outside your core-competence areas, demand more work from a player and therefore require you to put the team ahead of yourself. The funny thing is that you cannot hide your attitude from team mates. If you are selfish, you will be found out in no time at all. But if you are a team-player, the team will know and appreciate that as well.

Over the last decade a number of leagues like the IPL and the Big Bash have come up, each one bringing together international cricketers from many countries for just about two months. The IPL, in particular, with its unique format has brought in interesting changes to the traditional concept of a team. While the diversity in cultures, economic backgrounds and playing experience makes it a great learning experience for players, I must admit that there are challenges too in getting such a team to bond over such a short period. Normal team building tactics don't necessarily work here but if teams succeed in creating the right culture, the positives far outweigh the challenges.

The schedule, the travel, the sponsor obligations add to the intensity and pressure, making the IPL a very demanding tournament. Typically, international teams carry 14-15 players whereas IPL teams carry about 20-25 players. What this means is that the bench is much larger and given the format, could have some of the big stars on it. It can be frustrating for them sometimes and can even get to some players. It took a while for everyone to realize that a player's stated financial value is merely a reflection of the demand-supply situation and cannot be easily correlated to or has little to do with his ability. The team selection for the day is made keeping in mind the balance and the quotas and not the price that players have fetched in the auction. The pressure to perform is high but you need to think of the team at all times. If a player decides to play for himself, unlike in longer formats where other players can make up for one person's approach, such behavior could mean you could make your team lose. It requires a certain personality to understand and embrace this format. Being a team player is therefore even more critical and that is definitely something I consider while selecting players, now for the Delhi Daredevils or earlier for the Rajasthan Royals.

But like I said earlier, if you can get the team environment right, there is no better place to learn. Where else would a young bowler have got a chance to not only watch a great like Malinga train and play but to share a dressing room and listen to him share his knowledge! The camaraderie is amazing and it can only be good for the game.

In his book called *The Sacred Hoops*, Phil Jackson, the legendary coach of the Chicago Bulls, quotes Rudyard Kipling:

> *For the strength of the Pack is the Wolf and the strength of the Wolf is the Pack.*

That, I think, sums it up rather nicely.

RAHUL DRAVID

Acknowledgements

Long before this book was an idea, and to be honest it remained an idea for a long time, Mukul Deoras (then of Hindustan Unilever and later MD of Colgate Palmolive India) invited us to make a presentation at one of their events. 'The Winning Way', as we called the presentation, seemed interesting then and it is just as interesting today, 500 sessions later. So thank you for being the catalyst, Mukul.

Cricket and advertising have been an integral part of our life and the learning from those fields forms the basis of a major part of this book. We were helped by the fact that cricketers and other sportsmen, including Sachin Tendulkar, Virender Sehwag, Ian Chappell, Sanjay Manjrekar, Nasser Hussain, Viren Rasquinha, Ajinkya Rahane, Abhinav Bindra, R. Ashwin, Paddy Upton, Abhishek Jhunjhunwala and Virendra Sehwag agreed to speak to us. You will find their contributions at various points in this book.

Sport is just half the story. Almost all of the clients who invited us to their events were willing to talk to us about their organisations and the issues they faced. This helped us tailor presentations for them but also helped us draw the links between sport and corporate life better. Many of them, as you would imagine, were sports lovers and that made the dialogue easier. They provided the critical input for this book.

We specifically asked people to share their insights into management and corporate situations. Invariably and generously they said 'yes' and we were moved by how much time they were willing to give us. The who's who of corporate India have lent a weight to the book that it would not otherwise have acquired. So, a big thank you to:

Jaithirth (Jerry) Rao, former Country Head, Consumer Banking, Citibank India, and founder and former CEO, Mphasis

Nitin Paranjpe, Global President—Home care division, Unilever

Mukul Deoras, former MD, Colgate-Palmolive Co.

Niall S.K. Booker, formerly Chief Executive Officer, HSBC North America Holdings Inc

Subroto Bagchi, Co-founder, MindTree Ltd. and business author

Neeraj Garg, CEO, Apollo Health & Lifestyle

Sandip Das, Chairman and Senior Partner, Maitreyi Capital Advisors

Saugata Gupta, CEO, Marico Ltd.

Sunil Lulla, Chairman and Managing Director, Grey Group India

Shailesh Ayyangar, MD, Sanofi India

Anindo Mukherjee, Group CEO at Supermax Personal Care

Madhabi Puri-Buch, Member, SEBI

Marten Pieters, formerly MD and CEO, Vodafone Essar

Bharat Puri, MD, Pidilite Industries

Deep Kalra, Founder and CEO, MakeMyTrip.com

Vivek Kudva, Managing Director, India and CEEMEA, Franklin Templeton Investments

'Tiger' Tyagarajan, President & CEO, Genpact

Anand Mahindra, Chairman & MD, Mahindra Group

Ronnie Screwvala, Co-founder, UpGrad

Dr. Santrupt Mishra, CEO, Carbon Black Business and Director, Group Human Resources of the Aditya Birla Group

Sanjay Purohit, formerly MD, Levi Strauss India

Y. M. Deosthalee, Director & CFO, L&T Group

V. R. Ferose, Senior Vice President and Head of Globalization Services at SAP

N. R. Narayana Murthy, Co-founder, Infosys

Pramod Bhasin, Founder & Vice Chairman, Genpact

... and our closest friend and sounding board A. S. Ramchander, VP, Global Marketing, Castrol

Acknowledgements

In our first meeting with Gautam and Paul of Westland we knew we had found our publishers. It is a critical association for each must understand the other and we are very happy with them. They suggested that a young, enthusiastic, cricket lover, Karthik, be the editor. We went with that suggestion and it was a good one. Karthik is quick and has the ability to spot things that might otherwise slide by. It meant that we had to work a bit more after we thought the book was done but the extra effort has just made things better.

With the unfortunate shutdown of Westland, The Winning Way needed a new home to continue its success and we are thankful to Penguin Random House India and their Commissioning Editor Radhika Marwah for showing confidence in the book and ensuring it remains available to readers.

For the last word, for an excellent after mint, we wanted something from a great team player. Among his glittering and visible achievements, and others that numbers cannot make visible, Rahul Dravid can take pride in being an outstanding competitor and human being. Thank you Rahul, not for the first time, and maybe, not for the last.

So also, one day while thinking about who we could request to write the foreword, we thought we would be audacious and ask Mukesh Ambani. We have had an association through his wife Nita, as both our children have benefited from being at her excellent school. On the few occasions when we had met him, he had come across as being extremely down to earth and approachable. To our great joy, he said yes. We cannot thank him enough for this.

And so our book has Rahul Dravid and Mukesh Ambani in it. Life is good.

Notes

The Business of Winning

1. Personal interview with authors, September 2010
2. Interview on CNBC-TV18, November 2008
3. In response to e-mail questionnaire
4. In response to e-mail questionnaire
5. Personal interview with authors, September 2010
6. In response to e-mail questionnaire
7. In response to e-mail questionnaire
8. Personal interview with authors, July 2009
9. Personal interview with authors, December 2015
10. Personal interview with authors, April 2016
11. Personal interview with authors, July 2013
12. In response to e-mail questionnaire
13. Interview in *Outlook* magazine, August 2008
14. Personal interview with authors, December 2015

Goals

1. Personal interview with authors, July 2009
2. Personal interview with authors, May 2013
3. Personal interview with authors, September 2013
4. Personal interview with authors, September 2010
5. In response to e-mail questionnaire

6. Interview with *DNA*, June 27, 2010
7. Interview with *The Week in Chess* magazine, sourced from http://www.chess.co.uk/twic/linanand.html
8. In response to e-mail questionnaire
9. Personal interview with authors, July 2009
10. Personal interview with authors, July 2009

The Winning Triangle

1. Personal interview with authors, December 2015
2. Personal interview with authors, September 2013
3. Personal interview with authors, August 2013
4. Personal interview with authors, December 2015
5. In response to e-mail questionnaire

The Burden of Winning

1. In response to an e-mail questionnaire.
2. Personal interview with authors, September 2013
3. Sourced from https://www.brainyquote.com/quotes/quotes/w/warrenbuff383933.html
4. Personal interview with authors, January 2015
5. In response to an e-mail questionnaire
6. Sundar Pichai interview at Shri Ram College of Commerce, December 2015

Learning While Losing

1. Interview by Sujit John and Mini Joseph Tejaswi in *The Times of India*, September 9, 2010
2. Personal interview with authors, March 2014
3. Sourced from http://thinkexist.com/quotation/i-ve_missed_more_than-shots_in_my_career-i-ve/216033.html
4. Personal interview with authors, September 2010

5. Personal interview with authors, January 2016
6. Personal interview with authors, December 2012
7. In response to an e-mail questionnaire
8. Personal interview with authors, May 2015
9. Personal interview with authors, September 2013
10. In response to an e-mail questionnaire
11. Personal interview with authors, December 2015
12. Personal interview with authors, July 2009

Change

1. Sourced from http://www.goodreads.com/quotes/show/185636, accessed on 22/3/2011
2. Interview with the *Times of India*, February 24, 2011
3. Personal interview with the authors, July 2012
4. Sourced from http://thinkexist.com/quotation/he_who_rejects_change_is_the_architect_of_decay/208155.html
5. Interview in *Mint*, 18 October, 2016
6. Personal interview with authors, September 2010

Innovation

1. Personal interview with authors, February 2016
2. Personal interview with authors, December 2015
3. *The Daily Mail*, December 2014
4. Post-match interview, IPL 2011

Team Building

1. Personal interview with authors, October 2010
2. In response to e-mail questionnaire
3. Personal interview with authors, October 2011
4. Personal interview with authors, October 2010
5. From *The Independent*, October 14, 2002 sourced from http://www.independent.co.uk/sport/football/

international/mccarthy-ecstatic-after-keane-walked-out-613992.html
6. Conversation, November 2013

Leadership

1. Personal interview with authors, April 2010
2. Abhishek Jhunjhunwala Conversation Dec 2012
3. Deep Kalra Pers int Sept 2012
4. Paddy Upton Pers int May 2015
5. Personal interview with authors, May 2010
6. Personal interview with authors, July 2013
7. In response to e-mail questionnaire
8. Personal interview with authors, October 2010
9. In response to e-mail questionnaire
10. In response to e-mail questionnaire
11. In response to e-mail questionnaire
12. Personal interview with authors, July 2009
13. Personal interview with authors, September 2012
14. Personal interview with authors, October 2010

What Price—Winning?

1. Personal interview with authors, January 2016
2. Personal interview with authors, December 2015